TURNING UP

Taking Your SELF to Work

Thanks for turning up

03.02.26

TURNING UP

Taking Your SELF to Work

IAN HARRISON

First published in 2026 by Intellectual Perspective Press

To find out more about our authors and books visit:
www.intellectualperspective.com

Contents

Praise for Turning up: Taking your SELF to work

An inspirational exploration of the positive difference we can make to our communities simply by turning up for each other and valuing each other.

Aaron Hurst, Author of *The Purpose Economy*,
founder of the US Chamber of Connection

Taking inspiration from philosophy, psychology and his extensive work in this area, Ian has written a book which provides real insights into purpose, mission and authenticity at work. It's a must read for someone looking to thrive in the modern workplace.

Chris Daems, Host of the
Whatever Happens Next podcast

I sat down to read this book expecting a good solid read that I could take learning points from. What I received was an unexpectedly personal journey far beyond the rather trite "just be yourself". I now feel empowered to consider how we turn up as ourselves within our workplace communities – for each other and with each other – and how this impacts on the team and our business' ability to thrive within the local community. I will absolutely be using this book to revisit the themes and exercises through my career journey.

Alison White, Director, Broad Lane Vets

Turning Up is a powerful reminder that real 'success' in your work doesn't come from playing a part, putting on a show or the number of 'likes' on Social Media... it comes from showing up as yourself.

Ian makes a compelling case for true authenticity as the foundation of a meaningful career – whatever that may be. His insights challenge the idea that performance is about appearance, instead highlighting the impact of consistency, integrity, and being genuine. A must-read for leaders and teams, it's packed with practical insights, great questions and clear examples.

It's a valuable guide for anyone wanting to live their best life and help others to live theirs.

Karyl Iles, VP Arbonne International

AI is asking us some big questions, especially "What does it mean to be human?" This wonderful book provides generous insight and answers to that question. It demonstrates how purpose within a community is fundamental to human flourishing. I would highly recommend it to those both old and new to the workplace. It deserves to be required reading for anyone interested in humanity in their organisation.

Andrew Curwen, CEO, XLVets UK Ltd

This thought-provoking book made me think about things from a very different angle. I will certainly be applying the new perspectives it brings. Its direct and conversational tone made it engaging and accessible.

Tim Fawcett, Chartered Engineer

This book honestly feels like it was written for me. It cuts through all the surface-level "purpose talk" you hear in business and brings it back to something real.

What I love most is how it all fits together. It takes you on a journey from turning up as yourself, to turning up with meaning, to turning up together. It's the bridge between individual wellbeing and real business performance.

Liz Crutchley (she/her), CEO and Founder, Orange Orchid

This book is thought-provoking. It invites you to ask yourself the right questions and reflect on what truly matters. It's an easy read, yet deep and complex touching on subjects such as identity, mindfulness, human needs, community and the influence each of us carries in the world. It encourages to look within, to reconnect with your true self, and to show up more fully and authentically for yourself and for those you care about.

Camelia Cara-Ion, founder Wire Wise Book Club

TURNING UP
Taking Your SELF to Work

I am enough!

My life is not an advert, a performance, or a brand.
I am not perfect, but I choose to be present.

I choose to turn up.
Not to impress the world, but to change it.

I choose to see, and value you for who you are,
And create space for real connection.

This is our moment to turn up and be the difference:
One moment, one choice, one connection at a time.

SIKHONA
I am here to be seen

Thought experiments and bonus material

When I'm working with clients I make a distinction between stuff that is interesting, and stuff that is useful. In my head interesting stuff makes you pause and think. You might even talk to a friend about it later, but it doesn't make a difference. My aim is to deliver stuff that is useful – stuff that makes a difference. Writing this book was no different.

At the end of each chapter you will find a thought experiment. These are designed to enable you to play with the ideas in the chapter. How you use them is up to you: put the book down and play, make a note to play later or just carry on reading.

Each of these thought experiments and some other stuff is available to download as printable PDFs from www.Turning-Up.co.uk.

Introduction

What if the most radical thing you could do today was simply to turn up – as yourself?

You're showing up. You're working hard. You're trying to be a good colleague, a good manager, a good human. Perhaps you have reached a point in your career in which you are looking for work that will feel more meaningful. Perhaps you are facing a career change, or just looking for a workplace in which you feel recognised and valued. But something doesn't feel right; something is missing. You're tired, disconnected and unsure if any of it really matters.

Doesn't it seem strange to you that, with so much talk of purpose and connection, many of us feel disconnected and unseen? The world of social media is powered by the myth that everyone has a potential global audience. You can have 2,000 followers on Instagram and yet not be sure that anyone is actually seeing you. We live in a world that celebrates visibility, and that plays with words like "authenticity", "connection", and "presence". At the same time, we have a global pandemic of loneliness and people are searching for a deeper sense of purpose and reality in their lives.

The truth is that those who get "seen" the most on social media are not building genuine connections. Their interest is not in relationships but in followers that they can influence. Where social media has created success, it is in the broadcast and amplification of individual greatness. We're encouraged to curate, compete and conform. We're taught to polish our image, and to prove our worth. In this world, turning up is not about being present. It is about putting on a performance. We conform to our audience's expectations, and we become someone else's version of enough.

It is exhausting – and it is not real. Like empty carbs – we get an initial sugar rush, and then we need more. More affirmation from strangers and people with whom we have little genuine connection.

It's not just on social media – it's at work too. Constantly trying to fit in. Like actors on a stage, people see the character we have created, we enjoy the applause, and when we walk off the stage nobody really knows us. We are trapped by an image that we ourselves have carefully curated in order to fit in and be what we think others expect us to be.

This is your invitation to break the mould. An invitation to do something radical – to turn up at work as yourself; to see and be seen. You could keep chasing the next productivity hack, the next version of yourself. Or you could pause. Breathe. And ask: what if the most radical thing I could do today is simply to turn up – as myself?

Imagine a world of real connections. An ecosystem in which every individual is connected in a vital and dynamic way. You are not a lone tree in the midst of a woodland – you are an essential part of an ecosystem. Simply by being yourself, you are making a difference every day.

Head in the clouds and feet on the ground

I don't know where I first heard it, but someone once said that we should live with our head in the clouds, and our feet on the ground. We should dream big dreams, whilst staying rooted in reality. We should be pragmatic idealists.

When dreams lose contact with the ground they become fantasies. Ideals that can never be achieved. Dreamscapes into which we escape the less-than-ideal reality of our everyday experience. These fantasies don't inspire action. At best they provide an escape. At worst they become sources of depression, as life persistently falls short of the dream.

On 28 August 1963, Martin Luther King Jr. stood on the steps of the Lincoln Memorial and announced "I have a dream..." His dream was of freedom, equality and brotherhood for all. For over half a century his words have echoed around the world. A speech that was deeply rooted in the reality of the USA in the 1960s still reverberates. Has the dream been realised? Emphatically not. There are days when current societal trends leave me depressed by the determination of so many to make an enemy of the "other". But in the midst of the harsh reality of today we have moved forward from the societal norms of the 1960s.

For me Martin Luther King Jr.'s speech is the epitome of "head in the clouds, feet on the ground". He wasn't cowed by the enormity of the dream. He wasn't put off by the fact that the dream might never be fully realised (he was happy to have his head in the clouds), but he also knew that the dream could inspire real and immediate change (his feet were on the ground).

I wouldn't dare to compare this book with that great speech, but behind it is a dream. It is an ideal, but it is one that we can make steps towards. A dream that you can pursue, and a dream that, when pursued, can make a real difference to you and the people around you.

I want to invite you to stick your head firmly in the clouds and imagine a world in which human beings understand their interdependent relationship with one another and the world in which we live. A world where everyone is valued and everyone can flourish. A world in which the time we spend at work enriches and nourishes us as people.

I dream of workplaces where people like you feel seen and valued for who they are. I dream of a working life in which you experience belonging and safety in healthy workplace communities. I dream of teams that flourish in the knowledge of what they can achieve together, and that dream of changing the world for the better.

I also firmly believe that you and I can make choices that will take significant steps towards experiencing that dream. Even if you are not a manager or leader in your workplace, there is stuff you can do that has the potential to change your experience of the life you live at work. What is more – doing that stuff has the potential to change the way people around you experience the lives they live at work.

There are a set of choices that you and I can make that have the potential to revolutionise our lives and change the lives of others for the better. The best thing about it – those choices are profoundly simple (and simply profound).

Your invitation

This book is an invitation to pause. To breathe. To look again – not just at how you work, but at how you live, relate and show up. It's about rediscovering the power of being human in a world that often forgets what that means.

It is my hope that, in the pages that follow, you'll find a new way of seeing yourself, your work and the communities you're part of. We'll explore what it means to turn up – not as a polished product, but as a person. Not to impress the world, but to change it.

This is your invitation to be seen. To see others. And to make a difference – one moment, one choice, one connection at a time.

Community
Self-awareness
To see
BE
YOU
To be seen
Purpose
Meaning

Part one:
Turning up as your self

Are you ready to be the difference?

"Comparison says, 'Be like everyone else but better.'"[1]

Brené Brown

Fitting in and standing out

I've always believed that our greatest weaknesses are the flipside of our greatest strengths. This came home to me in a recent conversation with a friend. I should probably say that Ant and I both grew up in the pre-digital world. We are both now in our mid-fifties. During our conversation, Ant reflected that, in the main, our generation were brought up to frown on those who "blow their own trumpets". We were brought up with the idea that – if we worked hard – others would recognise our value and sing our praises. We chatted for a while and reflected that our experiences suggested that it simply wasn't true. If you want to progress, you need to blow your own trumpet. We also reflected that one of the ways social media has changed people is that we now live in a world where self-promotion is second nature.

For all the advantages of people learning to promote themselves, it's clear that this new reality comes with inherent dangers and challenges. It could even be argued that things have gone too far. We live in a world in which photographing your breakfast and sharing the picture on a public forum is normal behaviour. In a world in which so much of our lives are lived in public, it might seem odd to write a book about turning up. Isn't the problem that we turn up too often? The question is whether the digital age has taught us to turn up or to hide behind carefully crafted images?

The reality of our digital world is that we are constantly being encouraged to compare our lives with the projected lives of others. We are put under pressure to conform and feel the need to demonstrate how enviable our lives are. In her *Atlas of the heart*, Brené Brown puts it so beautifully: "Comparison is the crush of conformity from one side and competition from the other – it is trying to simultaneously fit in and stand out."[2]

The result is that when we do think about turning up it is often an image-centred consideration – how do I want to be seen in this context?

I asked ChatGPT what the idea of "turning up" means in popular culture. Here was the response:

"In popular culture, turning up (or turn up) generally means to party, have a good time, or get wild, especially in social settings like clubs, concerts, or celebrations. It's often associated with high energy, excitement, and sometimes indulgence in alcohol or other substances.

The phrase gained mainstream popularity through hip-hop and rap music in the early 2010s, with artists like Lil

Jon, Rae Sremmurd, and Travis Scott frequently using it in their lyrics. It can also mean simply bringing enthusiasm and energy to any situation, not necessarily in a party context.

For example:

- *"We're turning up this weekend!" → Having a big night out.*
- *"He always turns up on the court." → Performing with high energy in a game or competition."*

If this is correct, then "turning up" is about energy and enthusiasm. It is to invest all your resources in your current activity, whether that's partying or playing sport.

If you dig a little deeper, "turning up" can imply uninhibited self-expression. For some communities, turning up is not just about partying – it's a statement of resilience and joy in the face of adversity. This makes it a form of authentic cultural expression that resists narratives of respectability or restraint.

The problem is that in some contexts where people are encouraged to "turn up", the concept can be preloaded with specific expectations to behave in certain ways and those who don't conform are judged to be not "turning up".

The purpose of this book is to pull the idea right back to the concept of self-expression. Not in a forced or predefined way, but in a way that is real and true to your self. What does it mean for each of us to turn up as ourselves, with all our similarities and our differences?

Life-giving toxins

Cast your mind back to your early biology lessons. At some point you were told that we breathe in oxygen and breathe out carbon dioxide. Like many early science lessons, what we are taught is both true and not true. The truth is that pure oxygen is toxic to the human body. What we breathe is a nitrogen rich mixture of gases of which oxygen makes up just over 20%. In this context our bodies can extract the oxygen we need without encountering its toxic effects.

It strikes me that there is a form of self-expression that is toxic to ourselves and our community. I'm thinking of self-expression that takes no consideration of its impact. This is me, this is how I feel, you don't have to like me or to approve, and I don't particularly care whether my impact on you is positive or negative. There may be something authentic about this attitude, but there is also something toxic.

I want to turn up in a genuine way. I want your experience of me to be real and not a performance. I don't want to feel that I have to conform to be like you, or for you to feel pressure to conform to be like me. At the same time, I don't want to bulldoze you, to leave you feeling intimidated or less significant. In a real, meaningful interaction between two unique individuals both must leave space for the other. Both need to turn up, but we need to turn up in a life-giving way.

The connected individual

For as long as I can remember, I have been interested in the way people connect with each other. Over time, that interest has evolved into an interest in the well-being that flows from healthy workplace communities. Turning up implies a measure of self-awareness but it also implies a relationship with others. After all, no one speaks of themselves as turning up in an empty room. We turn up in the presence of others. We exist as individuals in community. Isolation is deadly to the human spirit, but so are communities that insist on conformity.

Taking your self to work

Much has been written about well-being at work. Around the developed world there has been a healthy recognition that employers need to create work contexts in which people can be well. Projects have focused on everything from the physical environment and nutrition to mental-health initiatives. All of which is great – in so far as it goes.

One problem is that many of these initiatives are cosmetic. Providing fresh fruit, or prosecco on tap, without addressing the fundamental issues that undermine wellness is the equivalent of creating a party on the decks of a sinking ship. The other problem I see is more controversial – we are in danger of ignoring individual agency. To put it bluntly – your environment will affect your mental health, but you also have a choice about how you respond to your environment. Don't fall into the trap of outsourcing your own wellness.

With all that in mind, we are going to ask: what does a healthy workplace community look like? What are the interpersonal dynamics of such a community? How can we turn up as ourselves and for each other? What does it mean to take your self to work?

Are you ready to be the difference?

The thoughts that follow are not intended to send you looking for the ideal workplace community, or worse, to give you grounds to complain about your current workplace community. My intention is to inspire and challenge you to embrace the possibilities that open up when you embrace the difference you can make and really turn up.

It's your choice – are you ready to be the difference? Are you ready to take your self to work in such a way that you become the difference for other people?

Being you matters

Well-being is one of those interesting ideas that we all instinctively understand but find difficult to define. It is more than being well. It is about the experience of our existence. To experience well-being is to flourish – to grow and to develop in a healthy way. According to Martin Seligman[3] there are a set of definable ingredients that come together to enable us to flourish – and they are all within our own control.

- We need to create times when we feel good. This is as much about our mindset and the way we manage our thoughts as it is about our environment.
- We need to understand what matters to us and how our life and work align with that.
- We need to build healthy, strong relationships.
- We need to reflect on what it means for us, as individuals, to live meaningfully.
- We need to define success for ourselves.

If you want to experience these five ingredients of flourishing, then you will need to explore four key things:

Understand what it really means to be you.

Find meaning in being who you are.

Discover the richness of the communities to which you belong.

Make a choice to be the difference.

As you develop the self-awareness to go on this journey you will experience a wide range of benefits. Those who do:

- are happier
- make smarter decisions
- have better relationships

- raise more mature children
- are better students
- choose better careers
- are more creative
- are more confident
- are better communicators
- perform better at work
- get promoted more often
- are more effective leaders
- are more enthusiastic employees[4]

In the words of Tasha Eurich: "self-awareness is the exquisite foundation to a life well lived."[5]

Being you matters for you.

It also matters for everyone else. Look back at the list above. Many of those attributes have an impact on the people around you. When we lack self-awareness, we lack clarity about our values and goals. We make poor choices, and we fail to understand the impact we have on those around us.

Knowing your "self" better is a key that unlocks so much of the value you can add to the world. It enables you to make deliberate choices to make a positive difference to the people around you.

We need you to be you.

Try this thought experiment:

Consider where you are expending your energy. What are the contexts in which:

- You can be an influence that has potential to make a positive difference in the lives of others.
- There is stuff you can control that would make a positive difference to the lives of others?

Spend some time to seriously consider the choice suggested at the end of this chapter. Are you ready?

ENDNOTES

1 Brené Brown, *Atlas of the heart*, 2021, Penguin, p.23

2 Brené Brown, *Atlas of the heart*, 2021, Penguin, p.22

3 Martin Seligman, *Flourish*, 2011, Nicholas Brealey Publishing, p.24

4 Dr. Tasha Eurich, *Insight: How to succeed by seeing yourself clearly*, 2017, Crown Business, p.4

5 Dr. Tasha Eurich, *Insight: How to succeed by seeing yourself clearly*, 2017, Crown Business, p.18

Being you

"Self-awareness is the exquisite foundation to a life well lived."[1]

–Tasha Eurich

It is often said that the value is in the journey not the destination. The journey I described earlier is a lifelong journey of discovery – an infinite loop – that leads to growth and wellness. It starts with a choice to "be you". But what does that mean?

As I sit and write these paragraphs there is a word that I find myself trying to avoid. It's a word that has become a buzzword in the world of personal development. As happens with most buzzwords it has lost much of its meaning. The word, of course, is "authenticity" and the problem with using it is brilliantly summed up by Peter York:

"For New Age, motivational, change-your-life speakers, marketeers, music entrepreneurs, foodies and design bugs – and, yes, politicians too – the idea of authenticity is nicely elusive, and very now."[2]

If you do an internet search for a definition of "authenticity" you will find these definitions in the Merriam Webster Dictionary:[3]

- not false or imitation: real, actual
- true to one's own personality, spirit, or character
- conforming to an original so as to reproduce essential features

You can see the problem – I can turn up authentically in the sense of being real, or I can turn up authentically as a copy of someone else.

"Authenticity" has been co-opted by those who want to sell a particular type of product, or image. It has become a shallow word that describes something desirable. A word that sells stuff. The word "authentic" has become strangely inauthentic.

Reflecting on a conversation with a young graduate, Yanis Varoufakis describes the pressure people are under to curate their identity as an authentic brand.

"For young people in today's world, even [self-ownership] has been taken away. Curating an identity online is not optional, and so their personal lives have become some of the most important work they do. From the moment they take their first steps online, they suffer... from two perplexingly contradictory demands: they are taught implicitly to see themselves as a brand, yet one that will be judged according to its perceived authenticity. (And that includes potential employers: 'no one will offer me a job,' a graduate told me once, 'until I have discovered my true self.')"[4]

This all-pervasive concept of personal branding has created immense confusion for people who are simply trying to understand themselves. What emerges is not authentic self but a carefully curated image that tries both to be bland – to suit the imagined average opinion – and to stand out – to get the attention required to get ahead. It is the very essence of the conundrum described by Brené Brown when she defines the nature of comparison: "Be like everyone else but better."[5]

As a society we find ourselves pulled in two very different directions. The magnetism of social media pulls us into a world that requires us to demonstrate how happy and fulfilled our lives are. Snapshots of the best moments of our lives are generalised into an idyllic impression of life, punctuated by rare moments when sad news acts as a cry for sympathy. Intellectually we recognise this effect and yet we all experience those moments when our own lives feel mundane in comparison to the lives we imagine others to be living. Comparing our self-identity to someone else's carefully curated brand, we feel ourselves to be insignificant, inadequate and without value.

At the same time, something deep within us recognises that what we aspire to is not real, that the images of constant success, happiness and fulfilment are, at best, partial. In response, something deep within us longs for something that is real; something that is true to "self" and the social need to feel that, when we meet, we get to see each other for who we really are.

In Zulu tradition there is a powerful greeting that goes like this:

"Sawubona" [I see you]
"Sikhona" [I am here to be seen]

In general usage these words can be used as lightly as we might say, "Hi! How are you?" They can also be used with a great deal of meaning. Used meaningfully, the word "Sawubona" is a greeting that acknowledges the individual's existence in the group. It captures a profound and common experience. We all, at some point, find ourselves in a situation in which we feel unrecognised, unacknowledged, invisible. We might say of such an experience, "I might as well have not been there. It was as if I didn't exist." Nobody saw us. To be greeted by the meaningful statement "I see you" is to know you exist in the minds of others, to know you matter, and to know that you are understood.

The response to "Sawubona" carries equal significance. "Sikhona" (I am here to be seen) implies a willingness to be present, to be open, and to contribute to the community.

In the two parts of this greeting is a social contract in which the group is mindful of, and values, the individual for who they are, and in return, the individual opens themselves to the group. To put it another way, the group creates a context of psychological safety in which the individual feels safe to turn up as themselves, to contribute and to benefit from the group without the fear of judgement.

The performances of a lifetime

It is beyond doubt that we all turn up in different ways in different situations. In my work, I use DISC profiling as a way to open up conversations about the way people's personalities present in the workplace. I always remind participants that these tools are time and context specific. That is, they are a snapshot of how someone's personality is likely to be showing up within a specific context at the time they complete the survey. It is not uncommon for a participant to make the kind of comment made the other day: "This is definitely me at work, but I'm very different down at the rugby club."

Is it inauthentic to be "very different" in different social settings? I do not think so. There is no moral obligation on us to make every aspect of our character visible in every setting. To do so would not be helpful or appropriate. And yet, I do want to turn up in way that is consistent with my sense of self.

Our word "person" comes from the Latin word "*persona*" which was originally used to describe the masks used in ancient theatre. Actors would play multiple characters, each represented by a unique mask.

Some scholars would suggest that it is through the different performances we put on that others get to know who we are, and we get to know ourselves.[6] It is probably important to understand that the idea being suggested here is not that we pretend to be someone we are not. Each "persona" (mask) is a true representation of a part of our self.

The joy of being your self

"Just be yourself. You'll be fine." At some time, or another, all of us have heard those words. We know they are meant to be encouraging. We know the subtext is that our encourager thinks we are great, we are enough. In their view, if people see in us what they see in us then everything will be OK – we'll get the job, we'll be accepted in the group. We know that is what is meant, but more often than not, those words send us into a tailspin. What on earth do they mean? How do you just be yourself?

Part of the problem can be the fact that we have never thought particularly deeply about what our "self" is. We have a sense that there is something we can each call "me" and we have a sense of whether we are being true to ourselves, or not. But we don't know how to just be ourselves. To "just be yourself" requires a journey of discovery into self-awareness.

In the pages that follow we'll explore ideas from an eclectic (possibly even eccentric) range of sources. We'll take inspiration from ideas from philosophy, religion and science. Our quest is not for "truth" but for insights that will help us to develop our self-awareness. The goal is not to define ourselves but to find ways to be ourselves.

The end game is captured in that beautiful greeting.

"Sawubona" [I see you]
"Sikhona" [I am here to be seen]

It is to be able to turn up with the ability and willingness to be seen for who we are and to see and value others around us for who they are.

Try this thought experiment:

Next time you meet with someone you don't know well, take time to "see" them. Push yourself beyond first impressions and be curious. Without subjecting them to twenty questions, find out about them, try to see them for who they are.In the same way, make a choice to be true to yourself. You don't need to show them everything, but make sure that what they see of you is really you. Be aware of the temptation to hide behind a mask or to pretend to be something you are not. Be you.

As the saying goes: "those who mind don't matter, and those who matter don't mind."

You might also like to google DISC profiling. You will have to pay for the best profiles but there are some lite versions that are free to use. If you do pay for a profile, I would recommend using a provider who will give you a personal debrief.

ENDNOTES

1 Dr. Tasha Eurich, *Insight: How to succeed by seeing yourself clearly*, 2017, Crown Business, p.18

2 Peter York, *Authenticity is a con*, 2014, Biteback Publishing, p14

3 https://www.merriam-webster.com/dictionary/authentic (Accessed October 2025)

4 Yanis Varoufakis, *Techno feudalism*, 2024, Vintage, p.177-178

5 Brené Brown, *Atlas of the heart*, 2021, Penguin, p.23

6 Steph Lawler, *Identity: sociological perspectives (second edition)*, 2014, Polity Press, p.116-137

You are bigger than you think

"Words can be misleading, and the deepest insights into the nature of reality are beyond the reach of language." [1]

Thich Nhat Hanh

If we are to turn up in a way in which we can be seen, and avoid the pitfalls of confusing turning up with personal branding, then we need to be willing to ask a profoundly simple question: what am I?

I choose those words carefully. I could have suggested that we need to ask: who am I? The problem is that the second question leaves us with nowhere to start. If I want an answer to this second question, I must start with the first. Asking, "What am I?" not only gives us a place to start, it leads to a point in which we can answer the more esoteric question: who am I?

What do you believe about yourself?

In exploring what it means to be yourself it is perhaps useful to start by dismantling some of the pre-existing ideas that may hold us back. We all carry with us a set of beliefs about the world we occupy. Based on our experience, our education and our upbringing, these beliefs enable our brains to function efficiently. They remove the need to think about everything as if it were new to us. The problem is that our beliefs can become outdated and can prevent us from experiencing the richness of life and achieving our potential.

Let's consider two examples. The first of which is trivial. The second less so.

It's Christmas Day 1977, and I'm trying to persuade my mum that I don't want the obligatory Brussel sprout with my dinner. I insist that ,"Brussel sprouts taste horrible!" My mum's reply was the same every year: "Have one, it's good for you, and you never know you might find you like it this year." Sometime later, sat around the table I grimaced as I ate the "horrible" little vegetable. But there is an interesting fact about Brussel sprouts – they are not the same today as they were in the 1970s. The varieties sold today have far less glucosinolate in them, and the result is that they are now a much milder tasting vegetable than the one on my childhood plate. My childhood belief that "Brussel sprouts taste horrible" is based on out-of-date information. This Christmas there will be at least three Brussel sprouts on my plate.

On a more serious note, most of us will remember being taught as children not to talk to strangers. This simple piece of advice has almost certainly saved lots of children from putting themselves in danger. In alerting children to "stranger danger" we enable them to form a belief – strangers are dangerous – that serves to keep them safe. For most of us as we mature this belief is modified and we learn to enjoy getting to know new people. For some, it turns into a sense of unease around people they don't know. When examined this unease is not based in any rationally identified threat, it is just an instinct they can't explain. The belief that "strangers are dangerous" has quietly morphed into "I'm not comfortable with people I don't know". Rather than serving to protect the individual, the belief now holds them back.

I'm not suggesting that everyone who finds meeting new people challenging has this underlying belief; any more than I am suggesting that it is immature not to like Brussel sprouts. What I am saying is that we all form beliefs and all of us, at times, are held back by beliefs that have outlived their usefulness, or which we misapply.

When a client is finding it difficult to break out from behind beliefs that are holding them back, I sometimes ask the following question: "In an ideal world what would you do?" The concept of an ideal world gives them permission to ignore the restrictions in their mind and to come up with possibilities that they otherwise wouldn't have allowed themselves to consider. It can be very effective but sometimes more is needed.

When we get stuck it sometimes requires the psychological equivalent of dynamite to blow through the blockage. Sometimes that dynamite comes in the form of an unexpected event that blows apart our preconception. Sometimes it can be a concept big enough to overcome our subconscious resistance.

Untangling the knot that was me

I was pacing up and down the garden talking to a friend on the phone. I can't remember what had started this particular conversation, but in the middle of it, there was one phrase my friend used that would prove to be incredibly liberating.

At the age of 40 I left a career in the church to begin a new part of my life as a business owner. I had spent nineteen years as a minister, and my identity had become deeply entangled with my job and untangling myself was a challenge. As I paced up and down the garden in the sunshine, I was explaining to a friend how that entanglement had left me feeling like I had nothing to offer in any other context.

"Ian, you need to realise that you are not who you are because you were a minister. You were a minister because of who you are."

Somewhere in my head the words pulled on a chord, and the knot that had tied my sense of self to my work began to untangle. To this day, I could still take you to the exact place I was on the patio when I heard those words. I was free to begin to explore who I am.

This starting place framed my exploration in a very specific way. I was determined that I needed to understand myself distinct from any job, activity or particular social context. I didn't want to go from defining myself by what I did in one job to what I was doing in a new job. I wanted to rediscover the joy of being "me" in a way that I could carry with me even if the external realities of my life changed. I needed something that would expand my boundaries and enable me to explore my friend's observation. I needed a stick of dynamite that would smash through the stuff that was holding me back. I found it, almost by accident.

An absolute statement of being

One day, I found myself reflecting on the Christian belief that we are made in the image of God. My mind then leapt to the thought that this God defines himself as "I am". By implication – he defies description beyond the truth of his existence. I began to reflect on what it would mean for me to simply say "I am". As I played with those words in my mind, I began to realise that when I say "I am" it means something different to when you say it. I am not you and you are not me. We are unique!

Energised by the path my mind was taking, I began to reflect on the multitude of descriptors that could describe my being. All of them were incomplete. None of them could contain me. My being cannot ultimately be defined by the words that I, or anyone else, use to describe me. I am more than any description can contain. The world renowned Buddhist monk and pacifist Thich Nhat Hanh put it like this: "words can be misleading, and the deepest insights into the nature of reality are beyond the reach of language".[2]

Let's unpack that for a moment. When we use the words "I am" we usually follow them with a descriptor. "I am a father." "I am a performance coach." "I am a Lancastrian."

Each of these descriptions reveals something about me, about my relationship to others, about what I do or about where I am from. Not one of them gets anywhere near describing who I am, and yet we can become hemmed in by these narrow descriptions.

I had become hemmed in by the statement "I am a minister." My identity had become intricately tangled with the specifics of the work. I felt like my job title contained my purpose, my way of being, my strengths. When I resigned, I could no longer say "I am a minister", but what else was I? Reflecting on those two little words – I AM – led to two conclusions:

- I was more than my job
- Whatever I did next would be an expression of me but would not define me.

The self without limits

There is one other implication of these two powerful little words – I AM. They are absolute and independent of outside authority. "I am" and I don't need your permission to be. I exist whether you acknowledge me or not. I am not limited by who you think me to be. "I am."

[Reread the paragraph above and make it your own. Read it as if you were writing it.]

You do not need anyone's permission to be. You exist whether anyone else acknowledges you or not. You are not limited by who others think you are.

A significant proportion of our "I am..." statements will be words that describe our relationship to other people. Some of these will be deeply rooted in social and biological imperatives. These are important ways of thinking about ourselves, but they don't get us closer to truly understanding ourselves.

To my children I am "Dad", but that word simply describes a family relationship. It tells you nothing else about me. It doesn't even help me to understand how I turn up as their dad. Perhaps most profoundly, I was who I am before I became a father. True, the relationship has shaped me as much as it has shaped my children, but I was not a blank slate formed exclusively within that relationship. I brought myself to the role and I learned and grew, but did it change my essence? Can I even say that I have an essence?

Health warning

This section should probably carry a bit of a health warning. In order to prepare us for later stages of our journey we need to ask a question that doesn't get asked often in the world of personal development. What is this "self" of which we want to be aware?

The challenge – and this is probably why most personal development books don't go there – is that there is no agreement. Religions, philosophers, psychologists and sociologists will give you any number of answers, but one of the endlessly interesting things about human beings is that when they think deeply about a subject they eventually hit on universal themes. They start with diverse world views and their ideas are framed by their particular way of thinking, but in the centre of the frame you will see ideas that are common to all.

This reality is not a thing!

In Zen Buddhism, nothing exists as a separate and independent thing, but that is not the same as saying nothing exists. Think of the book in your hands – it clearly exists. Now look closer, the book is made up of elements of other things. Without these other things, it wouldn't exist, and in that sense, it has no separate existence. The book is a formation made up of other things. In the same way, the self has an existence, but only as a formation made up of non-self elements.

This is the essence of the Zen Buddhist teaching about emptiness: to be empty is to be empty of self-existence but to be full of everything else.

Perhaps the most profound implication of this view of the self is that it is ever changing. It exists in this moment as a unique formation of everything else. If this is true, then self-awareness must be understood as a journey and not a destination. An infinite loop of discovery. You change, you learn, you grow.

I can't believe it's not me

Julian Baggini is a humanist philosopher whose thinking sits at the most materialist end of the spectrum, and yet his thinking overlaps considerably with that of teachers like Thich Nhat Hanh.

"The self clearly exists, it is just not a thing independent of its constituent parts." [3]

Julian Baggini

Where the two thinkers differ is in how they define "constituent parts". For Thich Nhat Hanh it is a universal statement – you are everything and everything is you. For Julian Baggini the constituent parts are internal to your own biology. Quoting the philosopher David Hume (1711–1776), he says that you are "nothing but a bundle or collection of different perceptions, which succeed each other with an inconceivable rapidity, and are in a perpetual flux and movement."[4]

According to this way of thinking, it is this inconceivably rapid and perpetual flow of perceptions that create a sense of continuity. From this sense of continuity comes a sense of self. The self as a thing in its own right does not exist – it is simply an impression, a way of understanding the highly complex stuff going on in your head. In other words – the existence of the self is a subjective truth. It exists because we experience it. On analysis, however, it is simply a trick of biology and has no absolute existence.

In trying to illuminate this idea, Baggini quotes the cognitive scientist, Douglas Hofstadter who describes the self as "a mirage that perceived itself, and of course it didn't believe that it was perceiving a mirage."[5] Another way of looking at it would be through the story of the film *The Sixth Sense*.

***If you haven't seen the film and want to avoid a spoiler, move onto the next section now.**

In the film, Malcolm Crowe, a child psychologist (played by Bruce Willis) works with a boy who can see ghosts. He helps the boy understand that his job is to help the ghosts find peace. The twist in the story comes with the revelation that Crowe himself is a ghost. Throughout the entire film, he interacts with the world of living without realising he, himself, is a ghost. The ghost perceived himself, and of course didn't believe that he was perceiving a ghost.

The ghost in the machine

The concept of ghosts is an interesting one and tells us a lot about the deeply rooted idea that there is a "me" that occupies my body, but which can exist beyond the existence of the body. These disembodied spirits are usually understood to retain the personality and essence of the individual who has died. The myths surrounding them are telltale signs that the cultures from which they arise have deeply held beliefs in the existence of the soul.

For those of us raised in this way of thinking it can be hard to let go of the idea of having a soul, and if not a soul, some undefined thing inside us that is "me". Some modern thinkers will point out that for all the exploration of the body and the massive advances in neuroscience we cannot identify this pearl within us. For them, this is conclusive evidence that there is no such thing as a soul. For those who choose to believe, such evidence is neither conclusive nor surprising.

Truth is not what matters here

If the question of whether, or not, there is something within us that we can call our soul (or even our "self") seems unanswerable to you, then Zen Buddhism provides a useful way out of the dilemma. Zen Buddhists divide truth into two categories. Samvriti satya (subjective truth) speaks to our experience and perception of ourselves, others and the things we encounter. In this sense how we perceive the world is true because it is the truth of our experience. On the other hand, paramartha satya (absolute truth) is there for us to grasp, and is capable of modifying our perceptions. Arguably, our goal should be to work so that our perceptions increasingly align with this absolute truth.

We never experience life in full ownership of the absolute truth, and we fill the gaps with stories and concepts that make sense of our experience. Whilst we hold them, these subjective truths are real to us, whether or not they can be objectively proven.

Understanding this is helpful in many ways. It legitimises and honours individual experience as being real. At the same time, it reminds us to hold our version of the truth lightly. Being aware that our truth is based on a partial understanding should leave us open to growth and change as our stories and concepts change in response to new understanding. Finally, it creates a ground for interaction in which different world views can meet, understand each other, and transcend themselves to become a deeper shared "truth".

I find this pragmatic approach to truth helpful in that it allows me to acknowledge the truth of my experience. There is something in me that I experience as my "self". I do not need science to find it within me. I do not need to objectively prove its existence. The self exists as an experienced truth, but need not exist as an objective truth. Whether or not I believe I have a soul makes very little difference to my lived experience.

With that thought we can unify the ideas we have been exploring:

1. *I am not just my body*
2. *The self is not a material thing or object*
3. *What I experience as my "self" consists of, and is shaped by, everything else*
4. *My experience of my "self" is real in that it is (subjectively) true*
5. *My experience of my "self" can change and grow in response to other "truths" that I encounter.*

Try this thought experiment:

Take a blank piece of paper, and in big bold letters, write the words "I am" across the top. Now complete the statement in as many ways as you can.

Use nouns (e.g. father, mother, son, dentist, explorer, homemaker) rather than verbs. Some people using verbs turn this experiment into an exercise in self-criticism. This is not the intention of the exercise.

When you have finished walk away for a few minutes. When you come back reflect on the words you have written. Do any of them fully describe who you are? When they are all put together, do they fully describe you?

No words can fully capture your essence – you are way bigger, way more than you think you are.

ENDNOTES

1 Thich Nhat Hanh, *The other shore*, 2017, Parallax, p.15

2 Thich Nhat Hanh, *The other shore*, Parallax, p.15

3 Julian Baggini, *The ego trick*, 2012, Granta Books, p.96

4 Julian Baggini, *The ego trick*, 2012 Granta Books, p.119

5 Julian Baggini, *The ego trick*, 2012, Granta Books, p.150

You are unique

"If you are always trying to be normal, you will never know how amazing you can be."[1]

Maya Angelou

With nearly eight billion people living on this planet, is it possible to claim that each of us is unique?

In the previous chapter we considered the idea that the "self" is not actually a thing in its own right, but a formation of other things – either of everything else, or of our biology. In this chapter we shall consider the ways in which we are shaped by the context in which we live our lives.

We begin life as part of a single biological structure that we share with our mother. For nine months we grow within her, becoming increasingly distinguishable in form and developing increasingly independent biological systems but ultimately connected by a temporary organ we call the placenta. In the process of birth we become biologically detached from our mothers and yet no less dependent on other human beings for our continued existence and growth. As we grow, and develop our sense of self, we are inclined to buy into the myth that we become independent, but it is probably more accurate to say we move from dependence to interdependence.

As a child develops a sense of “self”, it does so in reference to its parents and other significant people. As it ages the circle of significant others grows. So, a large part of our “self” is built on our relationship with others and an understanding of similarity and difference. We not only learn to compare ourselves with others, but we learn to see ourselves through the eyes of others.

Different and the same

The social psychologist George Mead made an interesting distinction between the part of the self that moves through the social world and exists in complex social relations (he called this part the “me”), and the part of the self that reflects on and interprets our experience and ultimately internalises our conclusions (he called this part the “I”).[2]

Mead’s insight is incredibly useful. He highlights the importance of understanding that the process in which we are shaped by our interactions with others is a critical process. The impact of these interactions is not ultimately determined by outside influences but by the conclusions we ourselves draw from them. We do not arrive in an interaction as a blank slate. We arrive with values, beliefs and a sense of who we are. This version of our “self” then interprets each interaction and is shaped by that interpretation. So, in the process of reflection and interpretation we inject something new, creative and innovative and it is that moment of creativity that serves to distinguish us from others.[3]

This creative tension between difference and sameness / uniqueness and commonality is interesting. Our sense of self modifies the way we experience the world, and our experience of the world modifies our sense of self. Self-awareness emerges then from a continual process in which we reflect on our lives and change according to our interpretation of our experiences.[4] This idea brings us to the interaction of continuity and change. An unending process in which our sense of self develops, grows and shifts over time and yet in which we perceive a continuity of remaining our self.

The birth of "me"

Returning briefly to George Mead's idea of the "I" and the "me" there is a question that must be answered. If it is the "I" that determines how we internalise our social experiences, where does the "I" come from? For Mead, the answer is clear. It is itself a product of social interaction.[5] As infants we initially take onboard the inputs from our earliest social interactions without much filtering at all. These early inputs then form the basis for our early reflections and interpretations and so begins a lifelong process in which we are shaped into the people we are and will become.

We should, however, acknowledge a differing (and arguably more widespread view). If we believe that there is an intangible essence that defines us, then that part of us which Mead would label the "I" has a different origin. Depending on your view, the "I" may be your soul, or it may be determined by your biology or something unique about your mind. If such a unique defining essence of self does exist, then even our earliest of interactions are interpreted by this original version of our "self".

Whether you believe there is an original essence that is you, or not, the reality would seem to be that from an early age we begin a lifelong process of change as we respond to the social interactions we experience. Understanding this leads to a conclusion that echoes the idea that the self is a formation made up of non-self elements. We are a formation of all our social interactions.

"'Without you I am nothing': without a nexus of others, none of us could be 'who we are'."[6]

Steph Lawler

Continuity and change

For me one of the thoughts that stands out among the ideas we have explored is the concept of continuity through change. Our identity is not founded in staying the same but in the perception of meaningful continuity. We saw that Zen Buddhists understand the "self" to be a formation made up of every other thing that exists. In this understanding every thing is in constant flux. We are constantly changing in an unending interaction with every other thing that forms our universe. Similarly, Julian Baggini suggested that our sense of self arises from an inconceivably rapid and perpetual flow of perception, and

Mead suggests we are constantly changing in response to social interaction.

Heraclitus of Ephesus, who lived 530–470 BCE, illustrated this idea when he pointed out that it is impossible to step into the same river twice. By the time we step in the second time, the water we originally stepped into has passed downriver. To all intents and purposes, the water of which the river consists is different. In the same way, as the river changes, so do you. So that, as you step into the river for the second time, not only is the river different but so are you.

"We both step and do not step in the same rivers.
We are and are not."

Heraclitus

If this idea of perpetual change is correct, is there any sense in which we are the same today as we were yesterday? Is the Ian Harrison editing this chapter the same Ian Harrison who wrote the first draft of this book?

Over time almost everything about us may change but – because we are not simply replaced in one fell swoop – each change becomes part of us before the next change. Our sense of self stays consistent and feels continuous.

One of my favourite memories of holidays with my children involved a visit to the Historic Dockyards of Portsmouth. The main attractions are two historic ships.

Now housed inside a purpose-built museum stands the remains of the Mary Rose, the flag ship of Henry VIII's navy. The incomplete original timbers were salvaged from the waters of the Solent in 1982. As your eyes trace the remains of the ship's decks, they look upon the actual wood across which the sailors walked on that fateful day in July 1545 when the ship sank. It is not a replica – it is the real thing – it is the Mary Rose. And, if you are a bit nerdy about history, as I am, it is thrilling to be in the presence of this piece of history.

Outside and across the dockyard another historic ship sits in dry dock. Every year over three hundred thousand visitors board Nelson's flagship – the Victory. To walk the decks of the ship that led the English fleet to victory at Trafalgar is a thrill, but the wood you are walking on is not the wood on which Nelson and his crew walked. Over time approximately 80% of the ship's timbers have been replaced. At no point was the ship scrapped and a replica built. Each timber replaced became part of the original ship. Now, even though so much of the timber was not at Trafalgar it can still be said to be the same ship that carried the body of Nelson home from Trafalgar in 1805. To walk her decks is to walk the decks of the original HMS Victory.

Where does all this get us? I think we can make three statements with which most people would agree regarding our experience of identity:

- *I am – and no one else is quite like me.*
- *I change. I am shaped by my experience of life, and I express myself differently in different contexts.*
- *I continue to be myself.*

The intangible me

We began our journey by unpicking ourselves from the limitations we and others create for us. I encouraged you to embrace the idea that you are unique and beyond the limitations of any specific definition. In doing so, my hope was that you would discover the joy and wonder of allowing yourself to simply be – embrace the joy of being.

"I am!"

I still get a buzz when I allow myself to revisit that thought. As powerful as that thought is, it requires grounding. In pursuit of this grounding we have considered four different but overlapping answers to the question "What am I?"

What stands out to me is that the part of us that makes us who we are is intangible. You will come to that conclusion whether you define that as an immortal soul, a unique formation that embodies every other "thing", or simply a construct of your biology. The search for the intangible "me" reinforces the ideas we explored in the previous chapter. To seek precise definition is to grasp at the wind. And so, we come back to a quote I used earlier:

"words can be misleading, and the deepest insights into the nature of reality are beyond the reach of language".[7]

And yet, language is all we have.

Try this thought experiment:

Imagine your life as a mosaic – a picture made up of coloured tiles. The tiles are different colours, shapes and sizes but each one represents something that has shaped you – a relationship, an experience, a cultural tradition, an influence, a value or belief.

- How does seeing your "self" as a mosaic help you appreciate your uniqueness?
- Which tiles are you most proud of? Which have been the hardest to accept?
- How does your mosaic change over time? What stays the same?
- How might your mosaic look different from someone else's? What do you share in common?

[If you like to think with a pen and paper you might like to draw the mosaic and label the pieces. As you label each piece consider how that piece has shaped who you are today. When the mosaic is complete, take a step back and notice the patterns. Notice the big influences and the more subtle influences. The things that make you similar to others and the things that make you different.]

ENDNOTES

1 Maya Angelou, Published on her twitter account (@DrMayaAngelou) at 4.45 p.m. on March 9th 2017
2 Steph Lawler, *Identity: sociological perspectives (second edition)*, 2014, Polity Press, p.5-6
3 Anthony Elliott, *Concepts of the self (second edition)*, Polity Press (Cambridge, 2010) p.33
4 Steph Lawler, *Identity: sociological perspectives (second edition)*, 2014, Polity Press p.6
5 Steph Lawler, *Identity: sociological perspectives (second edition)*, 2014, Polity Press p.6
6 Steph Lawler, *Identity: sociological perspectives (second edition)*, 2014, Polity Press p.17
7 Thich Nhat Hanh, *The other shore*, 2017, Parallax, p.15

Looking inwards

Mindfulness does not involve analysis or dwelling on things. It is simply noticing what we notice.

There is a problem at the heart of this book. If we accept that the "self" is ultimately intangible, how can we know ourselves? How do we even begin to access what it is to simply be "me"? Are we ultimately on a fool's errand, trying to touch the intangible and to define the indefinable? Why am I writing this book?

When people think about self-awareness, they often assume that it is to be found by looking inward. It seems obvious – doesn't it? But how do you do it? And what are you looking for when you turn inward?

In search of the intangible

We have explored a number of ideas about what the self is. Whichever view you take all of them present problems to the person who wants to look inwards to find themselves. For those who believe they have a soul, it is a non-material entity that occupies the physical body and contains the essence of who we are. What would you look for if you turned inward to find your soul? For those who believe they are formations made up of everything else, there is no thing to be found. This applies to the Buddhist view and the materialist view. In either case what would you look for if you turned inward to find yourself?

The famous psychotherapist, Carl Jung developed a complex set of theories to define the "self". He was driven by the desire to find a way for people to access the innermost parts of themselves. Whilst much of his work has been discredited, many of his concepts continue to inform our understanding of psychology.

One important distinction made by Jung was between "self" and "self-consciousness". His theory is complex, but put simply, he suggests that the "self" includes both conscious and unconscious aspects of our psychological processes.[1] In Jung's thinking the "self" is our "wholeness" and can never actually be fully known.[2] In a departure from his former teacher, Sigmund Freud, Jung uses the word "ego" to label the part of ourselves of which we are conscious. He suggests that the ego is "one's experience of oneself as a centre of willing, desiring, reflecting and acting."[3]

Despite their complexities, Jung's theories add some important ideas to our thinking about what it means to be "me". Like the other views we have considered, Jung understands the "self" to be intangible, even transcendent. One important concept he brings to the table for us is the idea that there is a significant part of the "self" that remains unconscious. The process of developing self-awareness is one of bringing the unconscious self into the light.

Jung called this process "individuation" – the conscious realisation and fulfilment of the self. An important part of this process is to explore and take responsibility for those parts of ourselves that we don't really want to look at – the shadow. We'll come back to your shadow later.

The problem with introspection

In an attempt to access the deep subconscious, Jung's theories led him to experiment with a range of methods. Most famously, he did extensive work on the interpretation of dreams. He believed that our dreams are products of our subconscious "self" that are, in large part, free from the controlling nature of the will. In other words, they are an almost entirely unfiltered expression of the subconscious.[4]

Jung's method of interpreting dreams is both too complex and too controversial for the pages of this book. Whilst analysing your own dreams may throw up some interesting thoughts it is probably an activity that should be handled with care. More recent research suggests that dreaming is part of the brains processing function in which it processes trauma and solves problems.[5]

Whilst the interpretation of dreams is intriguing, most people in search of increased self-awareness will turn to other forms of introspection. The question is how do we go about it?

When we set out to understand ourselves it is important to recognise that not all introspection is useful. In her book *Insight: How to succeed by seeing yourself clearly* Tasha Eurich identifies a number of pitfalls to be avoided:[6]

- Focusing on the process of introspection can lead to creating a story that gets us stuck. Instead focus on the outcomes or learning that comes from insight.
- Examining the causes of our thoughts, feelings and behaviours often leads to misleading answers. Instead of asking yourself "Why is this?", ask yourself "What is this?"
- Simply recording your unprocessed thoughts and feelings in a journal can lead to an unproductive spiral. Instead write less frequently and use your journal to process your thoughts and feelings and to make sense of them.
- Ruminating on our shortcomings and failures is a vicious, self-destructive cycle. Instead of self-flagellation, focus on what can be learned.

Sometimes the very act of analysing ourselves can become interference that holds us back from our potential. The key to understanding this is to ask yourself: what or who is informing your analysis?

Some years ago, I had the privilege of working on a project with Timothy Gallwey, author of the Inner Game series of books. In those books Tim identifies an internal voice that he calls "Self 1". This internal voice is a mental construct made up of the voices of everyone who has ever told us how we must, should or ought to do something, and when it is allowed to dominate it leads to rumination.[7] The hypothesis behind Tim's "Inner Game Theory" is that Self 1 gets in the way of learning. His method of coaching is focused on removing this interference to enable the player to practice a non-judgemental awareness of their game.

Awareness is curative

In *The Inner Game of Tennis* Timothy Gallwey describes the ability of the brain to learn for itself. The method Tim describes for learning and improving your tennis is best summarised in his own phrase "awareness is curative."

Stripping away the specifics of tennis, Tim's thesis is that as our brains are allowed to become aware of what is, they are more than capable of making changes. The key to this learning process is that it is not judgemental. It is not labelling what it notices as good or bad but simply noticing.

> *"It is difficult to become aware of the function of any pattern of behaviour while we are in the process of blaming ourselves for having a 'bad habit.' But when we stop trying to suppress or correct the habit, we can see the function it serves, and then an alternate pattern of behaviour, which serves the same function better, emerges quite effortlessly."*[8]

Essentially, he introduced mindfulness to the world of sports coaching and arguably laid the foundations of the performance coaching industry.

Mindfulness

When I first came across the word "mindfulness" it was being used as a synonym for meditation. Today we understand mindfulness more broadly and meditation practices (both religious and secular) are just one approach to mindfulness. What then do we mean by mindfulness?

Mindfulness is simply noticing things, without judgement or reaction. It is noticing our environment. Noticing how we are responding to our environment. Noticing ourselves – what we are thinking, feeling or doing. Mindfulness does not involve analysis or dwelling on things. It is simply noticing what we notice.

Whilst meditation is one route to mindfulness it is by no means the only route. One of my favourite ways of practising mindfulness is to simply go for a walk. Whilst walking I choose not to think about anything in particular, but to let my brain notice what it notices. Sometimes that leads to a relaxing walk noticing the flora and fauna around me, feeling the breeze or the heat of the sun, noticing the various smells in the air. On other occasions, something I have been working on comes effortlessly to mind and I see a way forward that I had not previously seen.

So often we are plugged into our music, the latest podcast, social media or emails. We fill every moment with stuff that occupies our mind and prevents us being present in the moment. Ellen Langers describes this condition as "mindlessness".[9] A really simple way of being mindful is simply to unplug yourself as you travel to work, or between meetings. Put your phone in your pocket, or bag, choose not to put your earphones in, switch off from the day ahead, and the noise of your home life and make a choice to simply notice what you notice as you travel.

Reconnecting with the moment

Practising mindfulness makes us alive to the moment in which we are living. It is a state of heightened awareness in which we are free from distraction to notice what is going on around us and inside us. We may notice thoughts and emotions related to the past or the future, but we don't engage with them, we trust that having become aware of them our minds will process them.

Thich Nhat Hanh describes the benefits of mindfulness as follows: "We recover ourselves, and we can encounter beautiful things around us in the present moment. The past is gone, the future is not yet here. If we do not go back to ourselves in the present moment, we cannot be in touch with life."[10]

What I notice

One of the most transformative habits I have learned came from being coached by a friend and colleague who often asks: "What do you notice?" The first time I was asked the question in a coaching session it surprised me. What am I noticing about my thought process? How do I feel in this moment? It is such a simple question, but it demands self-awareness. It stops you in your tracks and makes you reflect, and it does so without directing your thoughts to anything in particular. From being asked the question repeatedly in coaching sessions, eventually the words escaped the confines of the coaching sessions. Over time the question – "What do you notice?" – became a question that sits almost permanently in the back of my mind.

Embracing the intangible

We began this chapter by noticing the challenge of looking inside for self-knowledge. What is it we are looking for?

Over the years I have noticed various dangers arising from allowing others to guide us into this self-contained self-knowledge. One of these dangers is that we, or those guiding us, impose stories on us. We claim to be seeking knowledge of the self from within. What we do is impose stories and interpretations from outside.

When we seek to understand ourselves from the inside out we need patience. Our understanding will be emergent and slow. Mindfulness is not a quick root to self-awareness. It is an approach to life, and to a lifelong journey of learning about ourselves.

Try this thought experiment:

This is a simple experiment that I would recommend to everyone. Go for a walk and notice what you notice. If you can't leave your phone at home, then turn it off. No music, no predetermined focus, just walk with your eyes and ears open.

To quote Thich Nhat Hanh, "walk, not in order to arrive, but just to walk." Take your time. Allow yourself to notice your steps, your breathing, the feel of the breeze on your face. Notice your environment but don't dwell. Notice what you notice and move on, noticing other things as you move through the environment.

You can do this anywhere, but some suggest it is an easier habit to develop if you can get out of the bustle of your town / city into a quieter, less hectic environment.

ENDNOTES

1 Ruth Snowden, *Jung – the key ideas*, 2010, Hodder, p.67
2 Murray Stein, *Jung's map of the soul*, 1998, Open Court, p.151 – 169
3 Murray Stein, *Jung's map of the soul*, 1998, Open Court, p.15
4 Murray Stein, *Jung's map of the soul*, 1998, Open Court, p.49
5 Matthew Walker, *Why your brain needs to dream*, 2017, https://greater-good.berkeley.edu/article/item/why_your_brain_needs_to_dream (Accessed November 2025)
6 Dr. Tasha Eurich, *Insight: how to succeed by seeing yourself clearly*, 2017, Crown Business, p.97-126
7 W. Timothy Gallwey, *The inner game of tennis*, 1986, Pan Books, p.18-19
8 W. Timothy Gallwey, *The inner game of tennis*, 1986, Pan Books, p.67
9 Tasha Eurich, *Insight: how to succeed by seeing yourself clearly*, 2017, Crown Business, p.131
10 Thich Nhat Hanh: *Peace is every step*, 1995, Random House, p.11-12

Living from the inside out

We are not what we do, but we live from the inside out.

If working from the inside out is a slow, lifelong process, is there a quicker more accessible way of understanding ourselves? What if we were to start on the outside and work inwards?

Glimpses of the self in action

The choices you make, the work you choose, and how you go about it, are windows into your self. At times those windows are frosted and the image behind them unclear, and yet they all have something to reveal. Returning to George Mead's distinction between the "I" and the "me", the bit of you that is a unique formation is constantly responding to external influences. Those responses shape the career choices you make and the way you turn up in any given situation. We live from the inside out.

Given that what we choose to do is an expression of our "self", a powerful way to understand ourselves is simply developing an awareness of what we do, say and think and being curious about what that tells us about ourselves.

The mistake I made when I changed career was to attempt to draw a hard line between my past and my future. I could bore you with explanations of why I tried to do that, but it was a mistake, and it had the exact opposite effect to the one I wanted. My desire was to move on and embrace the new me, but the knot that tied my sense of self to my work could not be untied by treating my time as a minister as if it had no relevance or connection to who I am. Rather, I needed to reverse the frame and understand what it was about me that found expression in the work.

Before we consider how we might approach this outside – in exploration we need to be aware of the potential pitfalls on this journey.

The pitfalls of defining yourself by what you do

In a time when a lot is written about discovering your purpose, the idea of having a vocation might seem like the holy grail.

> Vocation (noun): vo·ca·tion
> : a summons or strong inclination to a particular state or course of action especially: a divine call to the religious life

---

I was 18 when I enrolled in theological college. At the time I didn't know what exactly I wanted to do but I was in search of a sense of a "calling". A couple of years later that "calling" arrived. Aged 20 I was appointed student-pastor of a small church in North Birmingham and by the time I graduated I had been asked to stay on as their pastor. I was 21, and I had no doubt in my mind that God had called me to a lifelong work. For nearly two decades I considered myself privileged to be paid to be what I was called to be. It was not a job, it was being myself and being paid to achieve my purpose. I had a vocation.

Then in 2008/9, after eighteen years of service, I realised that my internal resources were running low. For just under half my life I had done a job that was an extension of my self. Now in my late thirties, I was having to face the reality that I needed a change. After a long and painful consideration, I made the choice to leave the ministry. As I shared earlier, my sense of self, my sense of purpose, my self-worth had all been tangled up with what I had spent half my life doing. I had conflated what it meant to be "me" with "doing" a very specific work. Having chosen to walk away from that work it felt like I was no longer able to "do" me. I felt lost. I had become a human doing and lost sight of myself as a human being.

This story is not just my story. Over the years I have met people who have had very similar crises. Retirement, injury, redundancy, ill health or the closure of business can all lead to similar moments. Whilst most people will find their way through these crises, they are totally avoidable. We are not what we do, and rediscovering what it means to simply "be"' is something we can all explore.

Whether, or not, you have experienced this kind of crisis, the seeds of the problem fill the air around us. How often do we begin a social interaction with the question: "What is it you do?" To which the response is "I am a..." Notice the switch in language that comes so naturally:

"What is it you DO?"
"I AM a..."

Asked what we do we respond with what we are. Asked about activity, we respond with identity.

Of course, words are just words and I'm not suggesting that we become pedantic about these social interactions. What I am saying, is that we need to be mindful that the words don't creep up on us and don't start to become a definition of who we are.

You cannot afford to define yourself by what you do. The belief that there is a specific task you are on the earth to do is a potent drug but the comedown can be hard to handle. The key is to find our way to being ourselves whatever we are doing. Active human beings but never human doings.

Acting out of character

We are not human doings, but what we do provides a window into who we are. Put another way, we are not what we do, but we live from the inside out. Even when we might think of ourselves as acting out of character we are glimpsing something of ourselves.

We have all been there, driven by a need to fit in or to impress, we make choices, behave or speak in ways that create conflict within us. Sometimes that conflict arises immediately. Sometimes it arises later, as we reflect on our interactions. How are we to understand these moments in our lives? What is driving the conflict?

At the simplest level, we all form deeply held sets of values and beliefs. Values are the principles or standards that underpin the choices we make. They are fundamentally important to us. Our beliefs are the way we conceptualise our experience (remember my story about Brussel sprouts?). As we experience life these values and beliefs act as perceptual filters through which we interpret our experience. When we consider ourselves to have acted "out of character" we are often acknowledging that in some way we have behaved in a way that is contrary to our values and / or our beliefs.

Thought of this simply, noticing that we have acted "out of character" leaves us with a number of potential reflections:

- What drove us to this choice?
- What was so important about fitting in, or impressing, this social group?
- What is the value or belief we have contradicted?
- In what ways is that value / belief still valid or useful?
- How does this reflection help me to grow?

Whilst this simplistic approach has some practical value, it may be of longer lasting value to ask some deeper questions. We are not, after all, simplistic beings. Are we really acting in a way that is not true to our self, or is it that a part of our self with which we are less comfortable (possibly less conscious of) has expressed itself?

This is where Carl Jung's concept of "the shadow" is insightful.

The Shadow: "is an unconscious part of the personality that contains weaknesses and other aspects of the personality that a person cannot admit to having." It is "the dark side of our nature".[1]

Jung argued that the way forward towards wholeness was not to repress or ignore your shadow but to become conscious of it. With this consciousness we are able to make the conscious decision as to whether or not to allow our shadow to inform our choices, words and actions.

When we notice ourselves "acting out of character" there are two potential observations. We may have acted in a way that was misaligned with our values or a particular belief. When we notice this, we can revisit those beliefs and values to see if they are still serving us well. If they are, we can adjust our behaviour. If they are not, we can consider building a more useful belief or value. On the other hand, thinking of ourselves as "acting out of character" is sometimes not the most helpful observation. It may be that we are acting out of some darker, deeper part of our character with which we are uncomfortable, and which we have tried to suppress. In this case we need to own how we acted and, in doing so, learn to control ourselves in a more holistic way.

We are not what we do, but understanding what causes us to do what we do is a path to greater self-awareness.

Self-similarity

Some years ago, I became fascinated with fractals. These are never-ending patterns that repeat themselves at different scales. A property described as "self-similarity". As you zoom in on a part of the pattern you see smaller versions of the larger pattern. Mathematically, fractals are infinitely complex and yet produced by the repetition of simple processes. To add to the fascination fractals can be observed in nature.

The Sierpinsky triangle

A fern frond as an example of a fractal structure in nature

If you do a search of the word "fractals", you will quickly come across the Fibonacci spiral. Mathematically the spiral is constructed of quarter-circle arcs that dissect a set of squares. The length of the sides of each square is determined by adding the lengths of the previous two squares: 1,1,2,3,5,8,13,21...

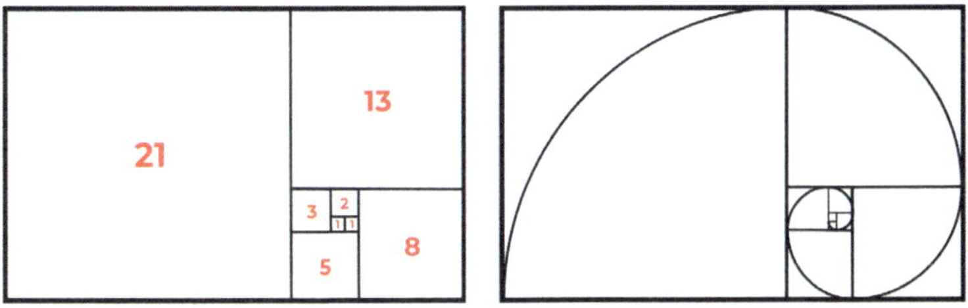

The spiral is also fractal, in that no matter how close into the centre you look you will see the same spiral. It becomes more fascinating when you realise that the spiral exists in nature – in the shell of a nautilus, the seed head of a sunflower, or the flower head of a Romanesco cauliflower.

As I explored the variety of infinitely complex fractal images, I began to realise that the Fibonacci spiral is a useful metaphor for the ways in which we show up as ourselves. When we are being true to ourselves then, at whatever level you get to know us you will see the same person.

This got me thinking about the different layers of detail at which we turn up as ourselves. As we have seen, we are infinitely complex, we show up in different ways at different times and in different contexts. And yet, in the pursuit of self-awareness it may be useful to think of the basic levels at which we express of ourselves.

I would suggest that we can think of ourselves at five levels of magnification:

- The contexts in which we find ourselves
- The adaptability with which we turn up in different contexts

- Our core personality traits
- Our drivers
- The intangible self

Each of these layers could be considered to be self-similar to the layer(s) beneath it. Each one providing an opportunity to develop our self-awareness.

The outer most expression of ourselves is our **context.** Or, more accurately, our contexts. The communities in which we find ourselves. The teams, networks and organisations we choose to be part of all express something about ourselves. What can we learn about ourselves from the places we find ourselves? Those in which we feel at home and those in which we feel uncomfortable?

Of course, we don't turn up in exactly the same way in every situation. There is **adaptability** in the way we express ourselves. We can turn up in ways that are true to ourselves without all of us turning up at once. What can we learn from the different ways in which we turn up in different contexts? What different aspects of ourselves do we notice? What explains the different ways in which we turn up and what do those explanations tell us about ourselves?

Zoom in further and we will find the ways in which we are always the same. We could describe this as our core personality. **The interface** at which our internal self finds external expression. These might be considered to be our personality traits, our preferences, the fundamental choices we make in life. What do we notice about ourselves at this level?

The next layer of magnification takes us to the internal expressions of our self. Here we could consider our **drivers.** The values, beliefs and passions through which we express who we are. What do these tell us about ourselves?

At the centre is **the intangible self**. That formation we have thought about, and which is so difficult to define as an entity in its own right. If we pull together all the observations from the outer layers, how do we understand ourselves? What becomes clear?

Seeing yourself through the eyes of others

Up to now we have emphasised personal reflection but there is another important perspective. How do the people around us see us? They cannot see what is inside us, but they see how we turn up, and if we can understand how other people see us, that gives us an alternate view on which to reflect.

"The bottom line is that self-awareness isn't one truth. It's a complex interweaving of information from two distinct, and sometimes competing, viewpoints"[2]

In seeking out this external perspective you need to be brave and sensible. Those people who will tear you apart out of jealousy, malice, or as an expression of their own stress, are clearly not good mirrors. Their motivation is not to provide helpful reflection but to vent their own issues. I have met leaders who have a deep fear of feedback that can be traced back to mishandled 360-degree feedback exercises.

Seek out those who care enough about you to give you honest feedback motivated by a desire to see you grow and flourish. Ask them specific questions and avoid overwhelm by focusing on a specific area in which you want to grow.

A thought experiment to try

Context: List the different contexts in which you currently find yourself.

- In which of these do you feel you belong?
- What is it that feeds this sense of belonging?
- In which do you feel you do not belong?
- What is behind this sense of not belonging?
- What does each of these contexts tell you about yourself?

Adaptability:

Thinking of the main contexts of your life.

- In what ways are you different in each context?
- In what ways are you the same in each context?
- In completing this exercise what could you learn about yourself?
- For each context: what difference do you like to make?

Interface:

Reflecting on your thoughts so far.

- Pulling together all of the answers to the last section, how would you describe yourself?
- How would you describe your personality?
- What do the choices you have made tell you about yourself?
- What preferences have you demonstrated?
- What do you feel passionately about?

Drivers:

Looking back over your previous reflections.

- What is it about the way you turn up that is important to you?
- What is important to you about the choices you have made?
- What "truths" explain why it is important for you to turn up as you do?
- What "truths" explain the choices you have made?
- Thinking of the things you are passionate about, what is important to you about these things?

The intangible self:

Take time to reflect on all your answers to the above questions.

- What have you learned about yourself?
- How would you describe yourself?
- How might these insights change the way you turn up?

ENDNOTES

1 Ruth Snowden, *Jung – the key ideas*, 2010, Hodder, p.68-69

2 Dr. Tasha Eurich, *Insight: how to succeed by seeing yourself clearly*, 2017, Crown Business, p.42

An absolute paradox

"The problem is not being aware of yourself but loving the person you find you are."[1]

Anon

Self-love is at the heart of healthy communities

So far, we have focused on knowing ourselves better in order to be ourselves, but there is one essential piece of the jigsaw missing, and that is the realisation that your community needs you to love yourself.

We are not talking about the narcissistic self-obsession that turns a person in on themselves and ultimately destroys them. As a defined personality disorder, narcissism is characterised by an exaggerated sense of self-importance and a need for influence and admiration.[2] This destructive self-obsession takes its name from the story of Narcissus who fell in love with his own reflection. Not realising that the reflection was himself, Narcissus suffered emotional agony at his inability to get closer to the perfect person he saw in the pool. You may see some analogies here in a society obsessed with selfies (sometimes achieved by an individual photographing their own reflection in a mirror).

In contrast to the destructive nature of narcissism, the self-love we are talking about is rooted in self-acceptance. When we accept ourselves for who we are, warts and all, and learn to love ourselves, it sets us free from self-obsession. We turn outward and extend the love we have for ourselves to those around us.

In the New Testament the whole law of God, as it relates to the way we treat each other, is summed up in the following words:

"You shall love your neighbour as yourself." (Galatians 5:14).

In this simple statement is implied a profound truth. You cannot love your neighbours unless you love yourself. The verse does not say love your neighbour more than yourself. It says you are to love them in the same way as you love yourself. Self-love unlocks our ability to love others. In this chapter we'll explore the ideas of self-acceptance and self-compassion. We'll consider ways in which we can respond to our ongoing journey of self-discovery and ask the question: how should we think about ourselves?

In answering that question, we need first to distinguish self-love from the popularist understanding of self-esteem and then consider what it really means to love ourselves "warts and all".

The pitfalls of self-esteem

American psychologist, Carl Rogers developed person-centred therapy. His approach was based on a belief that when a person is truly free to choose their goals, they will naturally select positive and constructive pathways. For Rogers, one of the keys to unlocking this freedom was "unconditional positive regard" – an attitude of basic acceptance and support regardless of what a person says or does. The intent behind this unconditional positive regard was that, free from judgement, the individual should be enabled to identify their shortcomings and to naturally learn from and even overcome them.

Later psychologists built on the influence of Carl Rogers and others to develop the idea of self-esteem. Canadian-American psychotherapist, Nathaniel Branden, defined self-esteem as follows:

"Self-esteem is the disposition to experience oneself as being competent to cope with the basic challenges of life and of being worthy of happiness."[3]

For Branden, it was important that self-esteem was grounded in reality. By 1997, twenty-eight years after publishing his book *The Psychology of Self-esteem*, he had become frustrated by the way the idea had become trivialised by popularist teachers and personal development gurus:

> *"Self-esteem is not a free gift of nature. It has to be cultivated, has to be earned. It cannot be acquired by blowing oneself a kiss in the mirror and saying, "Good morning, Perfect." It cannot be attained by being showered with praise. Nor by sexual conquests. Nor by material acquisitions. Nor by the scholastic or career achievements of*

one's children. Nor by a hypnotist planting the thought that one is wonderful. Nor by allowing young people to believe they are better students than they really are and know more than they really know; faking reality is not a path to mental health or authentic self-assurance. However, just as people dream of attaining effortless wealth, so they dream of attaining effortless self-esteem – and unfortunately the marketplace is full of panderers to this longing."[4]

Sadly, it is this trivial idea of self-esteem that is most prevalent: the idea that there is value in having a high opinion of yourself that is built on nothing more than a determination to have strong self-esteem.

"If I have to feel better than you to feel good about myself, then how clearly am I going to see you, or myself for that matter?"[5]

Kristin Neff

Psychologist Roy Baumeister applied this simpler and more popularist definition of self-esteem:

"[Self-esteem] is how people evaluate themselves"[6]

In 2003 he and his colleagues published the results of an exhaustive study in which they concluded that self-esteem was not "a major predictor or cause of almost anything"[7]

Here is the problem with ungrounded self-esteem: "Research suggests that we tend to think we're smarter, funnier, thinner, better-looking, more socially skilled, more gifted at sports, superior students, and better drivers than we objectively are."[8]

Paradoxically, alongside this tendency to overestimate ourselves, most of us are also prone to be very judgemental of ourselves. This, in turn can lead to feeling the need to boost our self-esteem. Here lies the danger inherent in the techniques promoted by those who offer us "effortless self-esteem." They offer a quick fix that is the equivalent to a caffeine fix or a sugar high. For a short time, you feel great about yourself but the comedown is both inevitable and hard. Self-esteem evaporates and is replaced by self-judgement. We start doubting ourselves and begin to feel that we can never be good enough. Kristin Neff, associate professor of educational psychology at the University of Texas, points out just how dangerous this approach to self-esteem is:

"The result of this line of thinking is sobering: millions of people need to take pharmaceuticals every day just to cope with daily life. Insecurity, anxiety and depression are incredibly common in our society, and much of this is due to self-judgment, to beating ourselves up when we feel we aren't winning in the game of life."[9]

"Self-acceptance means understanding our objective reality and choosing to like ourselves anyway"[10]

Tasha Eurich

When I don't like myself.

In the last chapter we briefly considered the idea that sometimes "acting out of character" arises not from being untrue to ourselves but from the emergence of our "shadow" – that subconscious dark side of our nature that we are sometimes loath to own. The reality is, that any journey of self-discovery will lead to identifying aspects of our self that we do not like.

When this dark side comes into view, we have a choice to respond in one of three ways. We can disown it and stick to phrases like, "I don't know what came over me, I was not myself." In doing so we reject the personal insight and push the undesirable part of ourselves back into the shadows where it waits for another opportunity to take us by surprise.

Alternatively, we could paint a picture of ourselves as victims of a part of our psyche over which we have no control – our very own Mr Hyde. A version of ourselves that we dislike, that we wish was different but about which we can do nothing. In this case we almost certainly will develop a self-loathing that is focused on our perceived shortfalls.

A third route is to own our shadows – to accept them as part of who we are and, in doing so, to master them. This third route is non-judgemental – we simply accept what we find in ourselves. This acceptance is not capitulation, it is knowledge, and that knowledge enables us to learn and to identify paths for personal growth that lessen the power of our shadow.

This brings us back to Timothy Gallwey's belief that "awareness is curative." By allowing ourselves to notice parts of ourselves with which we are uncomfortable, we open the door to change. It is important here to remind ourselves that the idea is that our "noticing" is free from judgement. It does not lead to us lecturing ourselves or feeling bad about our flaws. It is simply acknowledging their existence.

Closely related to self-acceptance is self-compassion – treating yourself with kindness and understanding. The key ingredients of self-compassion are all contained in the understanding we have been developing about ourselves.

You are a formation of many other things. We are the product of many influences: some good, some bad, some helpful and some unhelpful. Perhaps more accurately, we are the product of many highly nuanced and complex influences that have shaped us in different ways. Making us who we are – warts and all. This is not an excuse any more than it is a judgement. It is simply a fact. In the same way we might look on someone else and feel compassion because we recognise the circumstances that have brought them to where they are, so too we need to be understanding of ourselves.

You are a unique human being. In the words of Kristin Neff: "If we were perfect, we wouldn't be human; we'd be

Barbie and Ken – plastic figurines that look good but are also dead as doorknobs."[11]

When we notice aspects of ourselves we would like to change, we have a choice. We can allow our inner critic to remind us of our inadequacy, or we can choose to accept who we are in this moment. It is in allowing ourselves to notice our imperfections, to own them and then to choose to embrace ourselves that the magic happens.

The paradoxical theory of change

In her book, *Self Compassion*, Kristin Neff shares a formula that she adopted from a Buddhist teacher:

"Suffering = pain x resistance"[12]

According to this understanding, pain is a normal part of life. It is emotional or physical discomfort. Suffering, on the other hand, is the result of "comparing our reality to our ideals."[13]

In the context of self-awareness, pain is the natural experience of noticing things about ourselves that we do not like. On the other hand, suffering is the result of resisting the reality that knowing ourselves sometimes involves the painful acknowledgement of our flaws. This resistance manifests as our inner critic, our tendency to put ourselves down and to beat ourselves up. "Resisting pain truly is banging your head against the wall of reality... You are piling on feelings of anger, frustration, and stress."[14]

Beating ourselves up doesn't enhance our ability to learn and grow, it hampers it. We know that feeling calm, secure and confident opens the door to high performance and growth. Why do we think that is different when it comes to personal growth?

We have already seen the close relationship between self-acceptance and self-compassion. When we accept who we are – including all our flaws – we silence the inner critic who seeks to motivate us through fear of failure, and we create space in which to care for ourselves. We create space to love ourselves enough to want what is best for ourselves. We create an internal environment that can embrace change and growth.

Here then is the paradox that gave this chapter its title, personal growth and change is more likely when we accept ourselves for who we are right now. "If you care about yourself, you'll do what you need to do in order to learn and grow."[15]

How do you react when someone speaks harshly to you? What is your instinctive reaction? Like most people, I know that I respond defensively. Even if something in me recognises some validity in what they are saying, I will defend myself. The harshness of the criticism triggers my fight or flight responses. My body floods with adrenaline. My brain floods with cortisol. I am no longer in a physical state that can understand and process relevant feedback. I will defend myself (or run and hide).

Our inner critic provokes a similar response. We may recognise the validity of the criticism, but we also recognise the unkindness of the criticism. Rather than embracing the feedback we defend ourselves. We do not become more open to change, we become less open to change.

"Change occurs when one becomes what he is,
not when he tries to become what he is not."[16]

Arnold Bieser

It was this dynamic that was noticed by the psychiatrist Arnold Bieser when he wrote:

"Change does not take place through a coercive attempt by the individual or by another person to change him, but it does take place if one takes the time and effort to be what he is..."[17]

The inner critic holds us accountable to an ideal against which we fall short. The paradoxical theory of change says – this approach won't work. Instead, change is a natural organic process that occurs when we allow ourselves to be who we are in this moment.

If we are to grow, we can only start from where we are. I know that is a truism but sometimes we need to be reminded. Accepting who we are right now is the only place from which we can grow into the future.

A thought experiment to try

Health warning: This is possibly the hardest thought experiment so far.

Take time to reflect on the times when you have let yourself down. Perhaps, in certain circumstances there is a thing you do that leaves you feeling disappointed in yourself.

- What are the triggers?
- What leads you to do / say / think the thing that leaves you disappointed with yourself?
- What is that thing trying to achieve in the moment?
- What else could you do that would achieve the same thing?
- When you recognise you are in a situation that may trigger this thing you do, what could you do / say to yourself that would set you on a different course?

ENDNOTES

1 Cited in: Dr. Tasha Eurich, *Insight: how to succeed by seeing yourself clearly*, 2017, Crown Business, p.94

2 Dr. Tasha Eurich, *Insight: how to succeed by seeing yourself clearly*, 2017, Crown Business, p.86

3 https://nathanielbranden.com/on-selfesteem/ (Accessed November 2025)

4 https://nathanielbranden.com/what-selfesteem-is-and-is-not/ (Accessed November 2025)

5 Kristin Neff, Self compassion, 2011, Hodder and Stoughton, p.4

6 Roy Baumeister, *Rethinking self-esteem: Why nonprofits should stop pushing self-esteem and start endorsing self-control*, 2005, Stanford Social Innovation Review Winter, p.36

7 Roy Baumeister, *Does high self-esteem cause better performance, interpersonal success, happiness, or healthier lifestyles?, 2003*, Psychological Science in the Public Interest 4.1, p.1-44

8 Dr. Tasha Eurich, *Insight: how to succeed by seeing yourself clearly*, 2017, Crown Business, p.51

9 Kristin Neff, *Self compassion*, 2011, Hodder and Stoughton, p.6

10 Dr. Tasha Eurich, *Insight: how to succeed by seeing yourself clearly*, 2017, Crown Business, p.92

11 Kristin Neff, *Self compassion*, 2011, Hodder and Stoughton, p.71

12 Kristin Neff, *Self compassion*, 2011, Hodder and Stoughton, p.93

13 Kristin Neff, *Self compassion*, 2011, Hodder and Stoughton, p.93

14 Kristin Neff, *Self compassion*, 2011, Hodder and Stoughton, p.94

15 Kristin Neff, *Self compassion*, 2011, Hodder and Stoughton, p.165-166

16 Arnold Bieser, *The paradoxical theory of change*, 1970, https://ebrary.net/258652/sociology/paradoxical_theory_change (Accessed November 2025)

17 Arnold Bieser, *The paradoxical theory of change*, 1970, https://ebrary.net/258652/sociology/paradoxical_theory_change (Accessed November 2025)

Part two:
Turning up with meaning

Living meaningfully in the real world

"What matters, therefore, is not the meaning of life in general but rather the specific meaning of a person's life at a given moment." [1]

Viktor Frankl

I began this book with a challenge, or an invitation, to be yourself and make a choice to make a positive difference. I have suggested that in order to make that choice we need to know who we are. We've seen how we are shaped and how we shape ourselves and we have explored some ideas that enable us to reflect on who we are. We mentioned a Zulu greeting:

"Sawubona" [I see you]
"Sikhona" [I am here to be seen]

We cannot turn up in a way in which we are seen unless we have some sense of who we are. The more self-aware we are the more able we are to turn up in ways that are true representations of ourselves.

The next step on our pathway is to consider the way in which knowing ourselves unlocks insight into living meaningfully. Not driven by the apparent righteousness of a cause but driven by a sense of who we are, and what matters to us.

You won't get far today without running into a book, an article or a video in which you will be told of the importance of purpose in life and work. Western, post-modern culture is crying out to find meaning in our existence. Why are we here? What are we here for? Even if you initially answer those questions with reference to a religious faith, it is unlikely that your faith provides specific, personal answers to the question. The route to finding meaning is through understanding yourself.

Maslow has a problem

In 1943 American psychologist Abraham Maslow first proposed his now famous "hierarchy of needs". His basic theory is often summarised by the idea that the "deficiency needs" (physiological, safety, love / belonging, esteem) lower down the pyramid must be satisfied in order to free the individual to pursue the "growth needs" of self-actualisation. Maslow later clarified that this simplistic idea of upward progression through the hierarchy was not his intention, but he maintained the basic principle that satisfaction of the lower levels frees the individual to give more attention to the upper levels.

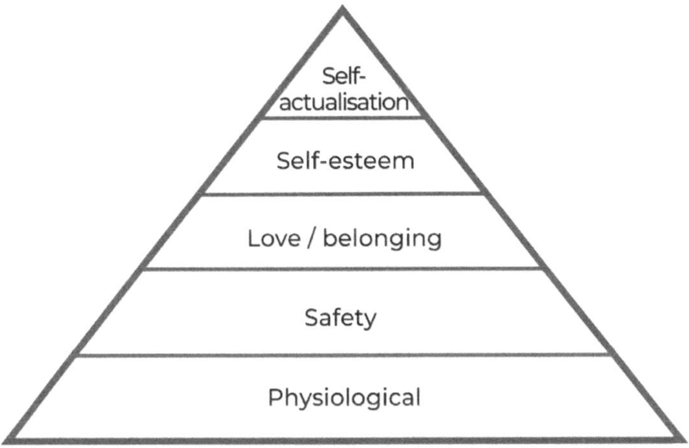

Between 2005 and 2010 a research project sought to test Maslow's theory in a way Maslow himself never did. With a sample of 60,865 people from 123 countries the research concluded that, if not met, the needs further down the hierarchy may demand attention but the existence of those needs does not prevent the pursuit and realisation of the higher levels.[2]

In other words, Maslow's hierarchy may accurately define the different types of need we experience, and it may have been successfully used as a motivational tool, but its underlying theory has been falsified.

It turns out that Maslow had based his theory on the analysis of a small sample of biographies; most of whom were accomplished, relatively wealthy, white men. It is a theory rooted in a wide range of assumptions about the superiority of wealthy advanced nations. Maslow has a problem.

When all you have is now

In stark contrast to Maslow's theory, the theories of Viktor Frankl flow from a very different experience of life. Frankl was a Jewish-Austrian psychiatrist who experienced the horrors of Nazi concentration camps and from his experience rethought the principles of psychotherapy. His starting place is almost the exact opposite to that of Maslow. Frankl's theories emerge from the experience of being stripped of everything except the moment in which you now live. A context in which none of Maslow's lower-level needs were met. In the concentration camps of Nazi Germany, the body underwent extreme deprivation, and everything was done to remove any sense of safety, love, belonging or esteem.

Frankl's experience in the concentration camps had taught him that everything we consider important can, all too quickly and brutally, be torn away. Even the spiritual and cultural traditions that so often provide meaning can be stripped from us. In the camps it even became impossible to live for the future. Freedom became an unimaginable goal and death a constant companion. Prisoners were left with a choice to live longing for the past or to find meaning in the present. Frankl observed that the former choice led to a loss of meaning and onwards to psychological and physical decline.[3]

Writing in 1962 Frankl argued that mankind was experiencing an existential vacuum. He suggested that in response to this vacuum we had capitulated to one of two dynamics: "comformism" in which we desire to do what others do; or "totalitarianism" in which we do what others tell us to do.[4]

What I find most interesting about Frankl's conclusions is the way Frankl sought to hold onto the lesson he had learned in the camps – to create meaning in the present moment:

> *"We needed to stop asking about the meaning of life, and instead to think of ourselves as those who were being questioned by life – daily and hourly. Our answer must consist, not in talk and meditation, but in right action and in right conduct. Life ultimately means taking the responsibility to find the right answer to its problems and to fulfil the tasks which it constantly sets for each individual."*[5]

Reality is mundane

One of my earliest memories of British TV in the 1970s was of my mum watching *Emmerdale Farm*. Originally a daytime soap opera, *Emmerdale Farm* dramatised farming not just as a job but as a way of life. The viewers' interest was in the rural way of life and the relationships of the Sugden family in the fictional village of Beckindale in Yorkshire (later renamed Emmerdale). By 1986 it was considered to be a sleepy programme in which not much happened, and the programme went through something of a reinvention. By 1989 it had been reinvented as a prime-time soap opera, now simply titled *Emmerdale*. New characters were introduced. Story lines became more dramatic and characters more colourful.

In the first fourteen years of the show the storylines involved two murders in the village. In the following thirty-five years there were twenty-six. One study analysed the murder rate in British soap operas and concluded that *Emmerdale*'s murder rate is 578,206% higher compared to the average murder rate in Yorkshire.[6] Alongside such a high murder rate, you will also find that in Emmerdale 68% of marriages fail,[7] compared to the UK wide rate of 42%.[8]

The evolution of *Emmerdale* storylines is typical of other soap operas. If they were real neighbourhoods you definitely wouldn't want to live in Emmerdale, Weatherfield (*Coronation Street*), Albert Square (*Eastenders*), or Hollyoaks.

Why are TV representations of life so exaggerated? Why is it necessary to have such exaggerated crime rates? Why do so many fictional marriages fail? The answer is as simple as it is obvious: normal life is not interesting enough to create dramas about. That's right – we are just too boring.

Of course, entertainment media and advertisers would try to convince us that life can be extraordinary. They create an idealised world and encourage us to aspire after idealised lives. At the same time the nature of social media makes us complicit in creating the fiction. We capture the extraordinary moments of our lives, the high points, the holidays. When we spend our hard-earned money on stuff an advertiser has told us will improve our lives, we quickly snap the picture and add to the fiction.

I'm not saying that life doesn't have its dramatic moments and its joyous occasions. I'm definitely not trying to be a killjoy. I just think we need to keep our feet on the ground. If we are to live meaningfully, it has to be in the real world.

In his essay entitled, "The case for a tragic optimism", Viktor Frankl describes pain, guilt and death as three unavoidable tragic aspects of life and argues that living a meaningful life cannot be contingent on avoiding these tragedies, or indeed on anything that can be taken away from us.

In the real world, life is mundane, it is tough, and it is finite. If we are to live authentically meaningful lives, then they must be lived here and they must be lived now. This moment is all we have. The past is gone, and the future is not here. The only place we can find meaning is here and now. Frankl, points us to three ways we can do that:[9]

- By doing something that leads to meaningful achievement or accomplishment.
- By experiencing something that elicits in us a love for the world in which we find ourselves. Or by encountering someone who elicits a loving response. This may be a loved one or a stranger.

- By facing unavoidable suffering with an attitude that transforms tragedy into triumph ("when we are no longer able to change a situation... we are challenged to change ourselves"[10]).

Reconnecting with meaningful survival

The first warning bells about Maslow's hierarchy went off in my head when I allowed myself to reflect on people I had met when working in Zambia. I was working with a charity that provided theological training conferences for church leaders who had not had the privilege of attending theological college. Many of them had been designated leaders simply because they were able to read. The conferences took place in far flung rural towns that were often an eight or nine hour drive from the capital, Lusaka. The people I met on those trips lived hard lives, many getting by on not much more than $1 a day. Being honest about myself, if I had been faced with their challenges I would have fallen apart. They did not. They demonstrated lives filled with joy and meaning. They were not ignoring their hardships; they were finding meaning and joy in the midst of them.

If you have spent time in the developing world then you may have had a similar experience. There is a culture shock and a challenge to the unconscious arrogance from which we form assumptions about what is required in order to live full, meaningful lives. I've never considered myself to be very materialistic but faced with people who have so little I was challenged by how psychologically reliant I am on "stuff".

Reflecting on these experiences I began to wonder if Maslow had got everything the wrong way round. That far from freeing us for higher things, having everything we need removes us from the stuff that really matters and disconnects us from the meaningfulness that is there in simply living day by day, moment by moment.

That is why I find Frankl's thinking so compelling. He shows us a way to find meaning that is not contingent on life going well, on having roofs over our heads, food on our tables, or even a future in which we can believe we can make a difference.

In the coming chapters we'll explore some ideas around how we can connect to a sense of purpose, and to particular missions. We'll explore the human need to feel like we are making a difference. Before we go there, my challenge to myself and to you is to reconnect to a sense of meaning here and now. To realise that our value as individuals, and the value of those around us is not contingent on a past that is no longer with us, nor on the potential to make a difference in an imagined future that may never exist.

Now is the moment in which you can make a difference. How you turn up in this moment; what you do now; how you respond to what you are experiencing now; how you respond to the people you are encountering now; your attitude in this moment towards the things you cannot change. These are the most profound opportunities to live an authentic meaningful life.

The challenge is profoundly simple: live well, do no harm, and when you can, do good for others. Now is the only moment there is. I have come to call this *meaningful survival* and to believe that it is the essential underpinning for a life well lived.

A thought experiment to try

Frankl challenges us to think of ourselves as those who were being questioned by life. He argues that meaning is found in taking responsibility to find the right answer and do the right things.

- What questions is life asking you today?
- How does each of those questions give you an opportunity to turn up as your self?
- How does each of those questions give you an opportunity to make a positive difference?

ENDNOTES

1 Viktor E. Frankl, *Man's search for meaning*, 2004, Penguin, p.113
2 L. Tay, & E. Diener, *Needs and subjective well-being around the world, 2011, Journal of Personality and Social Psychology, 101* (2), p.354-356.
3 Viktor E. Frankl, *Man's search for meaning*, 2004, Penguin, p.78-81
4 Viktor E. Frankl, *Man's search for meaning*, 2004, Penguin, p.111
5 Viktor E. Frankl, *Man's search for meaning*, 2004, Penguin, p.85
6 https://www.leeds-live.co.uk/news/celebs-tv/emmerdale-safest-village-soap-lowest-23555287 (Accessed November 2025)
7 https://www.dailymail.co.uk/femail/article-7055655/Emmerdale-crowned-divorce-capital-soapland-one-happening-189-episodes.html (Accessed November 2025)
8 https://www.ons.gov.uk/peoplepopulationandcommunity/birthsdeathsand-marriages/divorce/bulletins/divorcesinenglandandwales/2021 (Accessed November 2025)
9 Viktor E. Frankl, *Man's search for meaning*, 2004, Penguin, p.115
10 Viktor E. Frankl, *Man's search for meaning*, 2004, Penguin, p.116

Rethinking our place in the world

"You can't build a society purely on interests, you need a sense of belonging."[1]

Valery Giscard d'Estang

The world has never been more connected and interdependent. Never before has there been this potential to understand each other, to come together and to value each other. Why then are the global politics of the twenty-first century so divisive? Why are so many people feeling lost and alone? Why is there such an appetite for ideas like authenticity and belonging?

In our globally connected world, people are fighting for a sense of self, a sense of belonging and a sense of meaning.

Part of the problem is the size of the stage on which we are all actors. Arguably, our psychological make-up is not designed to operate in a global context. We may all be citizens of the world, but we are programmed to operate at much more local levels.

The psychologist Jeffrey Jensen Arnett identifies four psychological consequences of globalisation:[2]

- Most people develop a bicultural identity rooted partly in local culture and partly in their relation to global culture.
- Pervasive identity confusion (particularly among younger people) caused by people feeling that they don't belong in either their local or the global context.
- Self-selected culture – the gathering of like-minded people who feel the need to stand out from the crowd. These cultures may exist virtually more than they do in local contexts. Leading to a sense of loneliness in the "real" world.
- Identity exploration in love and work.

Arnett observes that "in order to unify people across these boundaries the values of the global culture necessarily emphasize tolerating and even celebrating differences. This means that the values of the global culture are defined in part by what they are not..." In other words, the diversity found among the world's population is so great that it becomes easier to define ourselves by what we are not. Which may help define what is unacceptable, but it leaves a vacuum when we seek out a sense of self.

The other conflicting, maybe even paradoxical, characteristic of global culture is that it has been driven by national cultures that emphasise individualism. People growing up in collectivist societies are increasingly embracing a significantly more individualistic view of life. The irony being that connection with the world is undermining the sense of connectedness in societies that have traditionally held a deep sense of interdependence.[3]

How then are we to understand who we are in a connected world? Is it possible to know ourselves, be true to ourselves and to embrace our connectedness?

In the chapters that follow, we'll explore our place in the world, its implications for how we understand ourselves and how we turn up for each other.

A personal Copernican revolution

The year is 1514 and a little noticed pamphlet is published that will begin a 200-year revolution that will change the way that a large part of humanity thinks of itself. It is hard to imagine from our standpoint that, for a significant portion of history, western civilisations had a very different perception of humanity's place in the universe.

They believed that the planet they occupied was the centre of the universe. The sun, moon and stars were understood to orbit the place where humans existed. In 1514 Copernicus published a pamphlet that suggested this might not be the case. Over the next two hundred years, others – like Galileo and Newton – would add their weight to the radical new understanding. Our planet, the place where we stand in the universe, is not the centre of everything. It is not even the centre of the one galaxy, among innumerable others, in which we find ourselves. Now we eagerly read news of the exploration of Mars and of the discoveries from orbiting telescopes that look out so far into the universe that they can be said to be recording the past as it happened. Scientists and educators are keen to place us as minutiae in the vastness of the universe. Far from the centre we look out at a universe of which we are but a miniscule part.

The lesson to be learned from this story is that when we put ourselves at the centre of our understanding, we are apt to misconstrue the reality in which we exist.

Despite our understanding of the universe, when it comes to day-to-day life, western thinking places the individual human at the centre of everything. It is an easy idea to buy into because it is our vantage point. We cannot help but see the world as being around us, but we must resist the idea that it revolves around us. The simplest of thought experiments will destroy the illusion and push us to consider a different perspective.

Imagine yourself observing the world around you. It is unavoidable for you to be the centre of all you observe. You turn on the spot and the world spreads out from the space you are filling. You are the centre of everything. But wait! As you look out from yourself you notice there are other human beings, each occupying a different space, each seeing the world from their own centre-point. And now you see the impossibility of the idea that the world revolves around you. Far from being the centre of the universe, you are simply an actor on an infinite stage with a unique, self-centred perspective.

A modern illusion

Our society loves nothing more than the story of a "self-made man", but it is a myth, a delusion. The "self-made" are formed on the backs of others, dependent on the hard graft of employees and suppliers. It is arrogant to believe that you put more into the system than you get out and, perhaps, that others are somehow less significant than you.

Imagine someone choosing to live alone, distanced from family or other nurturing relationships. This person can work remotely, earning money without committing to a workplace community. They can purchase all they will ever need online without interpersonal transactions. The illusion is of a man who is an island. Isolated and separate from the world.

Let's take a moment to examine the reality behind such a sad existence. We need only consider online grocery shopping. To the isolated individual it feels like independence, but it is far from it.

From the individual's perspective they sit down at their screen, and they choose their groceries. No one else is involved. There is no need to leave the house, and with the exception of a brief interaction with the delivery driver, there is no interaction with another human being.

Now consider the number of people whose work makes that "independence" possible. Imagine the number of people involved in the production and packaging of the food in a typical week's shopping. Consider the team of people who worked a night shift to stock the shelves. The person who arrived in the early hours of the morning to pick the specific order from the shelves. The team who stacked the crates of shopping ready for the driver to load their van before arriving at the door. From whom our "independent" loner receives his shopping, closes the door, and congratulates himself on his ability to live without being dependent on anyone else.

Behind this illusion of independence is a network of people that is far more complex than when previous generations walked down to the local shop to do their shopping. The reality of our sad, isolated individual is not that they do not need the community but that they have minimised their contribution to the community. The illusion is of self-sufficiency. The reality is one of absolute dependence and minimal contribution.

Ubuntu

There is a word that is common to many of the languages of sub-Saharan Africa. It dates back at least to the mid-to-late 1700s when the Zulu and Xhosa languages diverged, and is probably far older. It has come to represent a form of southern-African humanism. The word is "Ubuntu" and translates as "humanity to others" or "I am because we are."

UBUNTU: I am because we are.

Ubuntu is a recognition of practical and spiritual interdependence. "I am because we are." Notice the present continuous nature of this statement. But also notice that it is not “I am because YOU are.” It is “I am because WE are.” I am who I am because I am part of us. “I exist, and go on existing, because I am part of us.”

Notice also, the interdependent existence of both the individual and the corporate. Neither existing, nor able to exist, without the other. “I am because we are.”

The renowned Buddhist teacher, Thich Nhat Hanh speaks of us existing in a state of “interbeing”. To recognise our “interbeing” is to recognise how everything, and everyone, is dependent on everything, and everyone, else.

What I find fascinating is how these ancient understandings are reflected in our growing understanding of how the world in which we live works.

Thinking about boundaries – a moment of “enlichenment”

What is an individual? The word has the same root as the word “indivisible”. When we think of ourselves as individuals, we take a view of ourselves as distinct and separate from one another. It is the way we experience life, and it is a natural conclusion as we experience and observe our apparent independence. It is an undeniable, and shared, subjective truth, but is it the objective truth? Is there any sense in which we can consider ourselves as individuals?

Trevor Goward is a lichenologist associated with the University of British Columbia. He describes lichenology as a "discipline that can't define what they study".[4] Lichens were once thought to be plants, were then recategorised as fungi and today are understood not as a single organism but as a set of symbiotic organisms. At a simple level the structure of the lichens is fungal. The fungus, however, has no way of feeding itself. It lacks the ability to photosynthesise. What it does do is provide a stable context in which certain algae and cyanobacteria can exist. These "photobionts" live on the fungal structure and feed the fungus through their ability to photosynthesise.[5] Put simply the fungus provides a structure without which its residents could not exist and in return the residents feed their host. Each providing for the other. Each dependent on the other. Each part's existence subject to the other's existence. Ubuntu: "I am because we are."

The study of lichens raises a fascinating question: what is a living organism? Asking that question leads to what Goward describes as "enlichenment". That moment in which, as we consider the complex interdependence of lichens, we look up, we look around, and we realise that symbiosis is an all-pervasive characteristic of life.

The human biome

What is true about lichen is true about us. The microbes living in, and on, our bodies outnumber our human cells by a ratio of 10:1. These microbes are not simply hitchhikers, they are essential to our health. "The bacteria in the microbiome help digest our food, regulate our immune system, protect against other bacteria that cause disease, and produce vitamins including B vitamins B12, thiamine and riboflavin, and Vitamin K, which is needed for blood coagulation."[6]

"It is no longer possible to conceive any organism – humans included – as distinct from the microbial communities they share a body with. The biological identity of most organisms can't be prised apart from the life of their microbial symbionts... Our bodies, like those of all other organisms, are dwelling places. Life is nested biomes all the way down."[7]

"'We' are ecosystems that span boundaries and transgress categories. Our selves emerge from a complex tangle of relationships only now becoming known."[8]

Merlin Sheldrake

Failing to see the wood for all of the trees

Woodlands are evocative places. Perhaps it is the way their moods change as, in some places, the canopy all but shuts out the light, in others it allows shimmering pools of light to reach the woodland floor, and in others dappled light flickers through the canopy. These magical environments have long been the inspiration for stories of magic and mystery, of terror and of life-giving experience.

It turns out that they are far more magical than we ever realised. We have assumed that they are places where individual trees form, sometimes vast, groupings. With this understanding commercial forestry spent decades using various techniques to obliterate plants they considered to be "competitors" to the trees they were planting.

"...the thinking was clear and simple. Get rid of the competition. Once the light, water, and nutrients were freed up by obliterating the native plants, the lucrative conifer would suck them up and grow as fast as redwood. A zero-sum game. Winners take all."[9]

In *Finding the Mother Tree*, Suzanne Simard (Professor of Forest Ecology at the University of British Columbia) describes a journey of discovery that spanned over twenty years. Her research into the ecology of woodlands has revolutionised the way we understand these amazing environments. In her introduction she describes her findings:

"The trees soon revealed startling secrets. I discovered that they are in a web of interdependence, linked by a system of underground channels, where they perceive and connect and relate with ancient intricacy and wisdom that can no longer be denied."[10]

She goes on to describe a complex fungal network through which trees share nutrients, nurture their own seedlings, and pass chemical signals. Woodlands are far from being stands of individual trees competing for resources. They are complex ecosystems the success of which are dependent on the co-existence of the flora and fauna of which they are constituted. Woodlands are more like living organisms than groups of individual trees. Once again, our limited perspective had skewed our understanding. We saw a group of individual trees and called it woodland. We failed to see the interconnectedness and interdependence of the plants. We failed to appreciate that, far from being a group of individual trees, a woodland is an intricately connected ecosystem. It turns out that we really couldn't see the wood for all the trees.

In the same way that Trevor Goward suggests that the study of lichens raises broader questions about the nature of our existence, Suzanne Simard suggests that "Our own roots and systems interlace and tangle, grow into and away from one another and back again in a million subtle moments."[11] She goes on to draw lessons about our own ecosystem:

"A system is ever changing because its parts – the trees and fungi and people – are constantly responding to one another and to the environment."[12]

Human systems

If ever there was a time when we need to step back and see the wood, it is now. Humanity is not a vast collection of individual human beings. It is part of an ecosystem in which individual people, the diverse flora and fauna of our world, and the planet itself are intimately connected. As Suzanne Simard put it: "Our success in coevolution – our success as a productive society – is only as good as the strength of the bonds with other individuals and species. Out of the resulting adaptation and evolution emerge behaviours that help us survive, grow, and thrive."[13]

Words like "system" and "ecosystem" are the kinds of words that feel familiar, of which we have an instinctive understanding but which we may not truly understand. What do we mean when we use the word system? Here is a definition to get us going:

"...The essential properties of an organism, or living system, are properties of the whole, which none of the parts have. They arise from the interactions and relationships between the parts. These properties are destroyed when the system is dissected, either physically or theoretically, into isolated elements."[14]

In a system the components not only achieve more together they become something that they were not alone. They take on properties that do not exist in the individual components. They not only become capable of achieving more, together they become something that is more.

Living systems are not machines

So, a system is a coming together of parts from which emerge novel properties that do not exist in any of the parts by themselves. Even here there is a need for care. If we take a mechanistic understanding it will lead us astray.

"A mechanism is defined as a functional unity in which the parts of the mechanism exist for one another in the performance of a function. For example, a clock consists of a number of parts, such as cogs, dials and hands, and these are assembled into a clock, which has the function of recording the passing of time. The parts are only parts of the clock in so far as they are required for the functioning of the whole, the clock."[15]

We've all, at some time, "felt like a spare part," and in the mechanistic view of life it is possible to come to a point in which we are no longer serving a function. Applied to human systems in this way we also end up manipulating individuals to fulfil a role that we perceive is needed by the mechanism.

Mechanisms are governed by external laws that confine the system to fulfil specific functions. The temptation then becomes to treat human communities as machines that can be optimised through a system of rules and procedures. Not only is this dehumanising but it is apt to run into difficulties in the real world in which people are so much more than cogs in a machine.

When we work together we are not just capable of achieving more, we become something else, something bigger than any of us. Something life-affirming and dynamic – a human system.

Participation is not an option

There is another danger in thinking of the human system in this mechanistic way, and that is that we can be tempted to place ourselves outside of the system. We position ourselves as observers. When we do that, we can easily underestimate our influence.

There is a strange phenomenon in the world of particle physics that is worth our attention. It concerns a famous experiment that seeks to understand the behaviour and nature of light:

> *"Basically, waves that pass through two narrow, parallel slits will form an interference pattern on a screen. This is true for all waves, whether they're light waves, water waves, or sound waves.*
>
> *But light isn't just a wave – it's also a particle called a photon. So, what happens if you shoot a single photon at the double slits? Turns out, even though there's only one photon, it still forms an interference pattern. It's as if the photon travels through both slits simultaneously...*
>
> *The idea behind the double slit experiment is that even if the photons are sent through the slits one at a time, there is still a wave present to produce the interference pattern. The wave is a wave of probability, because the experiment is set up so the scientists don't know which of the two slits any individual photon will pass through.*
>
> *But if they try to find out by setting up detectors in front of each slit to determine which slit the photon really goes through, the interference pattern doesn't show up at all. This is true even if they try setting up the detectors behind the slits. No matter what the scientists do, if they try anything to observe the photons, the interference pattern fails to emerge."*[16]

You may, like me, find the physics a little mind boggling. Here is the takeaway for our journey: the act of observation changes the system. It is called "The Observer Effect": "The observer effect is the fact that observing a situation or phenomenon necessarily changes it."[17]

If you have ever experienced any form of observation or inspection in the workplace, then you will have experienced this effect first hand. The presence of the observer / inspector makes you a little nervous, your focus is affected (you cannot but help be aware of the observer), you second guess yourself more often, your self-talk escalates as you try to ensure you are doing things "right". At the same time, others involved in the activity are aware of the observer and are affected. Not only has the presence of the observer changed you, it has changed your environment. You are in an abnormal environment operating in an abnormal way – and all because someone is watching.

You cannot stand outside a system and observe it. Even if observation were your only function, it places you inside the system. You make a difference. You cannot change that fact. Participation is not a choice. The choice you have is what kind of difference you will make.

Choosing to have a positive impact

The choice each of us face every day is not whether, or not, we want to make a difference but what kind of difference we will make. What will our impact be on our family, our workplace community and on society. We are part of a human system in which we play an essential role. The way we turn up makes a difference in a thousand small ways.

We've all experienced those moments when someone's smile has been the pick-me-up that we have needed, and we find ourselves smiling – almost despite ourselves. For me this is one of the beauties of communities. When one person is struggling another is not. When I'm finding life a challenge, a kindly smile from someone else has the capacity to lift me up. It may not remove my challenge, or solve my problem, but it has the power to inject a moment of relief, a sense that I am not alone.

Every day presents us with a multitude of opportunities to make a positive difference in a multitude of small ways. The choice is ours as to whether we embrace those opportunities.

Be you and make the difference

In later chapters we'll pick up on ways we can think about discovering our purpose. We'll see that purpose is found in understanding who you are, what matters to you and what difference you can make to others. It's not hard. You don't need the universe to show you what it needs. Be who you are. Turn up with a deliberate intention to make a positive impact at every level.

Be yourself, and in being yourself make a positive difference to those around you – in your family, at work and in wider society.

And finally, take time to see the bigger picture:

Recognise that you are part of a system that embraces all of humanity, and the planet on which we live out our lives. Your well-being is dependent on that system and the way you turn up makes a difference to that system.

Be you and make a difference.

Try this thought experiment:

Next time you cook a meal or sit down to eat food, take time to think about how many people have been involved in getting that food onto your table. Think about the raw ingredients, the processing, the packaging, the transportation, the people working in the shop or delivering your food.

Broaden your thoughts to encompass everything else that makes your life what it is. Take time to be thankful for the way the system in which you live works.

Recognise that you are part of a system that embraces all of humanity, and the planet on which we live out our lives. Your well-being is dependent on that system and the way you turn up makes a difference to that system.

ENDNOTES

1 https://thinksmartpeople.co.uk/2024/08/creating-a-culture-of-belonging-empowering-individuals-in-the-workplace/#:~:text=You%20can't%20build%20a,Balancing%20Reactive%20and%20Proactive%20Approaches (Accessed November 2025)
2 Jeffrey Jensen Arnett, *The psychology of globalization*, October 2002, American Psychologist Vol. 57, No. 10, 774–783
3 Jeffrey Jensen Arnett, *The Psychology of Globalization*, October 2002, American Psychologist Vol. 57, No. 10, 774–783
4 Merlin Sheldrake, *Entangled life*, 2021, Penguin, p.101
5 https://britishlichensociety.org.uk/learning/what-is-a-lichen (Accessed November 202)
6 Marilyn Hair & Jon Sharpe, *Fast facts about the human microbiome*, 2014,The Center for Ecogenetics and Environmental Health, University of Washington (https://depts.washington.edu/ceeh/downloads/FF_Microbiome.pdf) (Accessed November 2025)
7 Merlin Sheldrake, *Entangled life*, 2021, Penguin, p.102
8 Merlin Sheldrake, *Entangled life*, 2021, Penguin, p.20
9 Suzanne Simard, *Finding the mother tree*, 2021, Penguin, p.92
10 Suzanne Simard, *Finding the mother tree*, 2021, Penguin, p.4
11 Suzanne Simard, *Finding the mother tree*, 2021, Penguin, p.180
12 Suzanne Simard, *Finding the mother tree*, 2021, Penguin, p.189
13 Suzanne Simard, *Finding the mother tree*, 2021, Penguin, p.189
14 Fritjof Capra and Pier Luigi Luisi, *The systems view of life: a unifying vision*, 2014, Cambridge University Press, p.65
15 Ralph D Stacey etal., *Complexity and management*, 2002, Routledge, p.20
16 https://www.popularmechanics.com/science/a22280/double-slit-experiment-even-weirder/ (Accessed November 2025)
17 https://ieeexplore.ieee.org/document/8423983 (Accessed November 2025)

Part three:
Turning up together

We belong together

"Belonging means your story is fully seen and valued... Belonging is being respected as an equal human being with full dignity."[1]

John A. Powell

To "Be You" – to turn up as your self – requires a level of self-awareness. In that self-awareness we can find meaning. Together self-awareness and a sense of meaning feedback into a clearer sense of what it is to "Be You". Now we are ready to journey out into the world, and to consider the workplace communities in which we turn up.

The need to belong is fundamental to our humanity. Buried deep in our genetic code is an understanding that belonging is necessary to our continued existence. When we feel like we do not belong our bodies produce a set of hormones associated with survival. Our stress levels increase, we become more alert to present threats, and we become defensive. When we feel like we belong a different set of hormones calms us down, reduces stress and enables us to become more sociable.[2] Deep within our brains, there is an instinctive fear that believes that if our community rejects us then we will die.[3]

To understand this clearly, we perhaps need to go back to simpler times when the family or tribe would hunt, and gather, together. In such a society the loner does not thrive. You are more likely to be fed if you are reliant on the combined resourcefulness of the group than if you strike out alone. To be isolated from the family / tribe was the route to a short and difficult life. True independence has never really been an option for human beings.

Belonging and conformity

In any bookstore there are shelves of books promoting various changes we can make to improve ourselves. Many of them involve encouragement to throw off the perceived shackles of repression imposed on us by others, or by society in general. The problem with this generalisation is that we fall into the trap of believing we are free from the influence of others when all we have done is change one set of influencers for another. The danger here is not in choosing a different set of influences, it is the way in which the belief that we are free from influence can serve to make us blind to the powerful new influences at work.

One of my childhood memories of growing up in Blackburn in the '70s and '80s is of the punks who would hang out by one of the fountains in the shopping centre. Punk culture was anti-establishment and non-conformist. The fashions and hairstyles were visual signals of the right to be and to do what you wanted to be and do. I'm sure many people in the movement genuinely believed themselves to have thrown off the influence of society and to have embraced just being themselves.

The problem with punk's underlying philosophy, and all other cultural drives for individualism, is that it was a con. If it had been a true commitment to individualism, you could have dressed like a rocker, rode a Vespa with the Mods and still been accepted as a punk. The reality, of course, was that the choice to identify as a punk meant a choice to conform to the social expectations that come with the label. To be a punk, or a Mod, or a rocker might have been to throw off many of the social influences of your parents and grandparents, but it was also to embrace the social norms of another social group.

There is a need to be more mindful of the influences acting on us at any time. We cannot escape from the influence of the groups with which we identify but we can develop a mindfulness that enables healthy analysis, interpretation and response to the constant flow of influence in which we live. This kind of mindfulness can enable us to be true to ourselves and to find those communities in which we truly belong.

What then is it to belong? Where and how do we find communities in which we can experience belonging?

Brené Brown makes an interesting distinction between fitting in and belonging. Fitting in is about assessing a situation and changing ourselves in order to be accepted. When we feel like we belong, we also feel free to develop our own distinctiveness. [4]

This idea is echoed by John Powell: "Belonging means your story is fully seen and valued... Belonging is being respected as an equal human being with full dignity."[5]

Powell's definition brings us back to the social contract implied in the Sawubona / Sikhona greeting. If to belong is to be fully seen and valued, and to be respected as an equal human being, then belonging requires us to commit to seeing others and to turning up so that we can be seen.

Belonging is about how we feel

As we begin to explore these ideas, we need to be clear that "belonging" is a subjective experience. Belonging is about how we feel. Those feelings are informed by a sense of connection, the belief that we are well regarded and that we are safe. These feelings may be influenced by our environment, by the attitudes and behaviours of the people in the community, but they are just as likely to be influenced by our own internal narratives.

This is why our journey began with self-awareness. To truly experience belonging we have to feel comfortable with who we are. In her book, *Braving the Wilderness*, Brené Brown asks two interesting questions:

- When it comes to belonging, what are people trying to achieve?
- When it comes to belonging, what are people worried about?

In summarising the outcomes of her research, she writes: "They want to be part of something – to experience real connection with others – but not at the cost of their authenticity, freedom, or power... Participants talked about their concern that the only thing that binds us together now is shared fear of disdain, not common humanity, shared trust, respect or love."[6]

We have heard this interplay between similarity and difference before. It is the heart of the contract implied in the greeting "I see you" – "I am here to be seen."

As individuals, then, we seek connection and recognition. We seek out communities with which we can identify, and yet within those communities we seek to be acknowledged for our uniqueness.

To connection and recognition, we might also add the idea of protection or care. We seek out groups in which we feel cared for. As Owen Eastwood put it: "To feel a sense of belonging is to feel accepted, to feel seen and to feel included by a group of people, believing that we fit in, trusting we will be protected by them."[7]

To understand this basic need is to begin to understand what brings people together, but it is not enough if we want to understand what creates a healthy community. A study of gang culture will reveal that street gangs provide these three basic needs. They provide contexts in which disenfranchised people feel connected – often by their shared sense of being victims of society – in which they feel seen, and in which they feel safe.

In *Tribal Leadership* Dave Logan and his collaborators define this kind of community as a stage-one tribe. “If people at stage-one had T-shirts, they would read “life sucks,” and what comes out of their mouths supports this adage. People at this stage are despairingly hostile, and they band together to get ahead in a violent and unfair world.”[8] These tribes are often characterised by self-centred and destructive behaviours. If individuals see an opportunity to get ahead at the cost of the tribe they will often take it.[9]

Despite these kinds of behaviours, it is important to understand that members of stage-one tribes still have a sense of belonging. In his book *Belonging*, Owen Eastwood quotes a former gang member describing what he found in the gang:

> *“This underlying sense of belonging mirrors unbreakable bonds. There is a feeling of euphoria that I am part of something, that people look at me and I have respect. I am a something. I am a somebody. The thing I got out of it was the loyalty of another brother next to me in good times and bad.”*[10]

This dysfunctional form of community, drawn together in a sense of shared victimhood, echoes the fear expressed by participants in Brené Brown's research: "Participants talked about their concern that the only thing that binds us together now is shared fear of disdain, not common humanity, shared trust, respect or love."[11]

So, we crave belonging that is grounded in positive commonalities, that is confident and open-hearted. We crave communities in which we trust and are trusted, in which we feel respected and able to respect others, and in which we feel loved and able to love. When we can't find this kind of positively charged community our need for belonging may push us into communities that are far from good for us. Communities bound together by fear and a shared sense of victimhood. Communities in which we are respected for as long as we conform. Where love is conditional and self-serving.

The good news is that in the research done by Dave Logan and his colleagues they found very few stage-one tribes in the workplaces they studied.

Try this thought experiment:

When you think about belonging to a workplace community (either your current community or your ideal community):

- What does belonging to a workplace community give you?

Thinking about the workplace community of which you are a part:

- How did you come to be part of that community?
- What attracted you to it?
- What could you do to increase your own sense of belonging?
- What could you do to help others to feel that they too belong?

ENDNOTES

1 John A. Powell, *The power of belonging*, 2024, Sounds True, p.97

2 Owen Eastwood, *Belonging*, 2021, Quercus, p.23

3 Daniel Coyle, *The culture code*, 2019, Random House, p.12

4 Brené Brown, *The gifts of imperfection*, 2020, Hazelden Publishing, p.35

5 John A. Powell, *The power of belonging*, 2024, Sounds True, p.97

6 Brené Brown, *Braving the wilderness*, 2017, Random House, p.33

7 Owen Eastwood, *Belonging*, 2021, Quercus, p.22

8 Dave Logan, John King and Halee Fischer-Wright, *Tribal leadership*, 2011, Harper Business, p.18

9 Dave Logan, John King and Halee Fischer-Wright, *Tribal leadership*, 2011, Harper Business, p.19

10 Owen Eastwood, *Belonging*, 2021, Quercus, p.22

11 Brené Brown, *Braving the wilderness*, 2017, Random House, p.33

Healthy workplace communities

"If we are constituted through our interrelatedness with others, then it is only in connection that the individual properly understood comes alive."[1]

John A. Powell

We all need somewhere to belong, and given how much of our time is spent at work, we want to feel that we belong in our workplace community. That means we are looking for a community in which to work that is grounded in positive commonalities and is confident and open-hearted. We want to be able to trust and feel as though we are trusted. We want to be respected, and able to respect others. Dare I say it, we want to feel loved and be able to love.

Before going any further it may be useful to define terms. There are probably three words being used with a measure of overlap. They are "tribe", "team" and "community".

Let's start with the simplest of these. A team is a group of people who are brought together to fulfil a specific function. We can use the word at various levels of granularity. Smaller businesses often refer to their entire workforce as "the team". Once the business reaches a certain size, functional teams begin to form and, if not managed carefully, these teams can begin to think of themselves as siloed units, even internal competitors.

Teams are defined by their functional purpose, they do not necessarily become communities or tribes. The use of these two words is far more confused. In "Tribal Leadership" a tribe is defined as follows:

"a social unit, bigger than a group but smaller than a society."[2]

Whilst the words "tribe" and "community" may be used interchangeably I think Charles Vogl and Carrie Jones make a valuable distinction:

"Charles still identifies as a returned Peace Corps volunteer. Charles also still values international travel, cultural sharing, and serendipitous adventure. And he thinks that there are moral and respectful ways to explore foreign cultures, as do most Peace Corps volunteers. However, given that his Peace Corps service ended years ago, he is not active in a Peace Corp group that shares mutual concern between himself and other returned volunteers. There is such a community in the world, but he is just not a part of it now. He considers his relationship to other peace core volunteers as tribal."[3]

For Jones and Vogl, a community is "a group of people who share mutual concern for one another."[4]

Christine Porath identifies the same quality when she says:

"I define a community as a group of individuals who share a mutual concern for one another's welfare... They often include duties or obligations, and members may share ideas, interests, proximity (remote or not), or any other number of things, but a distinguishing factor is caring for one another."[5]

I have chosen to use the word community because, in my mind, it implies something deeper than the functional nature of a team, or the shared identity implied by the word "tribe".

Having settled on the word "community", it still seems necessary to speak of "healthy communities". We all know that teams, tribes and communities can exist in name without meeting the needs we have identified. A healthy community then is one that can be described as follows:

A healthy community:

- is a group of people who share mutual concern for one another
- is a group of people among whom individual members feel recognised and safe
- is a group of people who hold a shared identity based on whatever factor has brought them together
- is a group who share a positive outlook on life

Let me try to pull this together into a working definition of a healthy workplace community.

A HEALTHY WORKPLACE COMMUNITY IS A GROUP OF PEOPLE, DRAWN TOGETHER IN THE CONTEXT OF AN ORGANISATION, WHO FORM A SHARED IDENTITY. TOGETHER THEY FEEL RECOGNISED, VALUED AND SAFE.

Becoming us

A key phrase in our working definition of a healthy workplace community was that its members *form a shared identity*. In his introduction to *Concepts of the self*, Anthony Elliott writes: "collective identity gains its power through the establishment and recognition of common interests."[6] These are found in shared experience, shared purpose, or simply liking the same things. What is important to notice is that a shared identity does not necessarily involve the loss of personal identity but rather the existence of social identification. John Powell reminds us of lessons learned from people like Suzanne Simard when he writes: "if we are constituted through our interrelatedness with others, then it is only *in connection* that the individual properly understood comes alive."[7]

To have shared identity is not to become identical but to recognise meaningful points of contact. Understood like this, we can see how we can each belong to multiple communities. We can also see how each of us enriches the communities to which we belong through the interaction of both our similarities and our differences.

One of my daughters and her husband enjoy the world of medieval re-enactment. On a number of weekends every summer, they can be found on various fields dressed in period costume and armour re-enacting various historic battles from the Wars of the Roses. In a recent conversation with my son-in-law, he reflected on how hobbies like re-enactment bring together groups of people who have nothing else in common other than the focus of their shared hobby. That one aspect of sameness is enough to create a sense of shared identity, from which spring the relationships that lead to a sense of belonging.

In recent years it has been our habit to take the short drive to witness the re-enactment of the Battle of Shrewsbury and to visit our daughter in her medieval habitat. Mixing with the re-enactors, what quickly becomes apparent is how different members of the group add their own unique contributions. Different personalities, different preferences and different perspectives add colour, diversity and creativity to the group. Drawn together by sameness we enrich each other with difference.

Our identities are transformed through our relationships and the magical dynamic of communities that leads to what Ralph Stacey refers to as "the simultaneous emergence of individual and group identity."[8]

Exclusivity

In some ways the very act of defining something is exclusive. A definition tells us what something isn't as much as it tells us what something is. In the same way a community is, by definition, an exclusive group. You are either part of the community, or you are not. That does not mean a community cannot be welcoming, have permeable boundaries and even be open to redefining its boundaries, but it will always define those who are inside and those who are outside.

Here lies one of the dangers of group identity. It plays out in every playground, in interest groups, in workplaces and pretty much anywhere people gather. When outsiders are looked down upon, or identified negatively as being "other," group identity quickly becomes toxic. Once again, John Powell provides some insight: "the problem comes when that [shared] identification is reduced to something singular, static, or essential."[9]

You don't have to know me for long before you'll discover that I am a lifelong fan of Blackburn Rovers who currently play in the Championship division of the English Football League. Fifteen miles down the road from Ewood Park, where Blackburn play their football, you arrive at Turf Moor, the home of Burnley Football Club. The two sides are bitter rivals and, even when playing in different leagues, the fans of each side sing about their hatred of the other. For many this "hatred" is mere football banter but for too many it is personal and real. For these people their identity as fans of their team is so exclusive that they are not willing to acknowledge other points of contact and similarity.

A healthy community, then, is one that has clarity around its defining characteristics – particularly around its shared centre of gravity – but which also embraces the value that its members bring with them through their belonging to other communities. Human society is best understood as a network of networks, or perhaps a community of communities. You may not be able to be a fan of Blackburn Rovers and Burnley but you can be a fan of Blackburn Rovers whose best friend is a fan of Burnley, who belongs to a hiking club most of whose members think football is a waste of time, and who works in a national team made up of people with a wide range of personal connections with many different interest groups.

Once again John Powell puts it very succinctly: "Bridging becomes more likely to occur if we can lean into the many identities we carry. In addition to such a space offering more possibilities to connect, in this space we may be less prone to fear and anxiety. The other may be different and at odds with me on some or even many things, but if I remain open to exploring our multiplicities, we have a much greater chance to find or create space where we can bridge with or without agreement." [10]

Try this thought experiment:

Consider the variety of personalities, backgrounds and interests represented in your workplace. Narrow your thinking down to the people you work with directly.

- How different is their story from yours?
- How do those different stories create the possibility of different insights?
- What different interests do people in your team have?
- What do they do with their personal time?
- How does this variety enrich the team?
- Given your unique story, in what ways can you add richness to the team?

ENDNOTES

1 John A. Powell, *The power of belonging*, 2024, Sounds True, p.92
2 Dave Logan, John King and Halee Fischer-Wright, *Tribal leadership*, 2011, Harper Business, p.24
3 Carrie Melissa Jones and Charles H. Vogl, *Building brand communities*, 2020, Berrett Koehler, p.16
4 Carrie Melissa Jones and Charles H. Vogl, *Building brand communities*, 2020, Berrett Koehler, p.2
5 Christine Porath, *Mastering community*, 2022, Balance, p.xiii
6 Anthony Elliott, *Concepts of the self (second edition)*, 2010, Polity, p.14
7 John A. Powell, *The power of belonging*, 2024, Sounds True, p.92
8 Ralph Stacey etal., *Complexity and management*, 2002, Routledge, p.182
9 John A. Powell, *The power of belonging*, 2024, Sounds True, p.93
10 John A. Powell, *The power of belonging*, 2024, Sounds True, p.125

The way work works

In a healthy workplace community, everyone makes a difference.

In the last chapter I proposed the following definition of a healthy workplace community:

A HEALTHY WORKPLACE COMMUNITY IS A GROUP OF PEOPLE, DRAWN TOGETHER IN THE CONTEXT OF AN ORGANISATION, WHO FORM A SHARED IDENTITY. TOGETHER THEY FEEL RECOGNISED, VALUED AND SAFE.

To this we can add another idea we have explored – healthy workplace communities are human systems in which we not only achieve more together, but we become something new. Something that has properties that do not exist in any one individual. We not only become capable of achieving more, together we become something that is more.

Some time ago I found myself working with a leadership team of about fifteen people. In one exercise I asked them to choose a service they offered and map out the customer journey. Each step of the journey was written onto a Post-it note, starting with first contact all the way to a satisfied customer who has paid their invoice. I then asked the group to identify which team, or individual, was responsible for each step of the journey.

The service they had chosen to map was quite technical and there was a nervousness among one or two in the group that perhaps they had chosen something that would not include many teams / people. I encouraged them to carry on with the exercise and to see what happened.

Having identified the teams / people responsible for each step, I asked the group to step back and see what they noticed. One of the technicians in the group was first to speak:

"When we picked this service, I was concerned it wouldn't be inclusive enough. It is very technical. Now I'm looking at this – the technical team are only on one third of the Post-its. Something I thought of as very technical couldn't be done without every team in the business."

Needless to say, the conversation that followed involved significant expressions of mutual appreciation.

On another occasion I was working with a small business of about twenty people. Some worked in the office, others were remote, some were full-time, others part-time. I asked them to look at their key tasks and identify what they needed in order to complete those tasks. Having done that, I asked them to identify where the "supplies" came from – who in the team provided them with what they needed to complete their tasks. Together we then created a network map showing the interdependencies within the team.

Once again, I asked what people noticed. One of the part-time workers, who worked almost entirely remotely spoke up: "I hadn't realised so many people relied on what I do! I've always thought of myself and my work as a bit of an outlier and yet pretty much everybody has connected back to me."

This time the conversation that followed involved members of the team expressing appreciation for the work done by their colleague as people sought to reassure him of how important he was to the team.

Both these situations arise from people becoming tunnel visioned with respect to their own role. In the first situation the technician had lost sight of how important all the other functions in the business were to enabling the central function. In the second story, one individual in a small team had lost sight of the impact his work had on everyone else.

This blindness sometimes arises from perceptions of status and the historic language that reinforces the hierarchy. In professional services there is a historic language in which client facing service providers are designated as "fee earners". These are the people who are seen to bring the money in, and their bonus structure is often structured around this function.

Thankfully this language is beginning to die but it remains persistent and is worth debunking.

In the "good old days" a solicitor, or similar professional, would set up an office and build a practice entirely based on their network. Marketing activity consisted of the professional joining various societies and clubs and being seen in all the right social contexts. Even then, the idea of "fee earners" was flawed. As the professional sipped their sherry there was almost always a secretary in the background grinding out the admin. Without the secretary the professional's ability to be out and about would be severely limited.

Fast forward to a modern professional practice. What would the impact on income be if you stripped out all the receptionists, the accounts team, the HR department, the marketing department? The answer, of course, is that the practice income would quickly collapse. Those who are designated "fee earners" are simply the front end of a fee generating system.

Every business is a community of people, gathered together around the objectives of the business. Work works, because of this interdependent network. In a healthy workplace community, we transcend the abilities we have as individuals and achieve amazing things.

If we are to see and be seen at work, then we have to recognise the value each person brings to the community – including ourselves. In a healthy workplace community, everyone makes a difference.

Synergy

SYNERGY [noun]:

the combined power of a group of things when they are working together that is greater than the total power achieved by each working separately

---

If you have ever worked in a team that comes together in the way we have described, you will know how special it is. The magic that happens is often described as "synergy" – when the combined power of the group exceeds the total power that would be achieved if everyone worked separately.

Synergy is the holy grail for workplace communities. It is the reason teams exist, but calling a group of people a team doesn't necessarily create synergy. Whilst there are any number of reasons why teams fail to function effectively, there is one fundamental issue that guarantees their failure.

Let me state this boldly: individualism will always lead to dysfunction in a team or community. When we perceive ourselves to be a gathering of individuals, we immediately create problems. We create the potential for competition for status. We create the potential to undervalue each other. We underestimate the value others bring to the table.

In their book *Tribal Leadership*, Dave Logan, John King and Halee Fischer-Wright describe what they label as a stage three tribe.[1] These tribes are made up of individuals in pursuit of personal greatness. Their allegiances are self-serving and last for as long as the tribe is perceived by the individual to maintain or enhance their personal greatness. According to the research behind the book, 49% of workplace tribes in the United States fall into this category. Less than 24% of workplace tribes rise above this individualism to achieve something more.[2]

There is no "I" in TEAM (or is there?)

We've all heard the saying that there is "no 'I' in TEAM" and we have probably all instinctively warmed to the idea. We understand that the intention of the phrase is to point out that self-centred attitudes and behaviours can destroy teams, and with that we can all agree.

However, we have considered the idea that a healthy community is one in which we feel recognised and valued. As Brené Brown put it: "True belonging doesn't require you to *change* who you are; it requires you to *be* who you are."

In this sense, a healthy team is not one in which the "I" is absent but one where it is embraced, and in which we are all able to be who we are. In a healthy team the sense of "us" is discovered in the interplay between our similarities and our uniqueness.

Beyond synergy

Workplace communities are human systems. Ralph Stacey suggests that the best way to understand these systems is as "complex adaptive systems":

"a complex adaptive system consists of a large number of agents, each of which behaves according to its own principles of local interaction. No individual agent, or group of agents, determines the patterns of behaviour that the system as a whole displays, or how those patterns evolve, and neither does anything outside of the system."[3]

He later concludes that "in this new paradigm, an organisation becomes what it is because of the intrinsic need human beings have, individually and collectively, to express their identities and thereby their differences."[4]

In other words, the human systems we call workplace communities are constantly adapting and evolving in line with the complex interactions between the individuals who make up the system. In particular, this evolution and adaptation is driven by the need for each of us to both express our individual identities and our shared identity as a group. To express both our similarities and differences.

Freedom

One of the most hypnotic sights in nature is to watch a murmuration of starlings fill the early evening sky. These flocks of birds form over mass roosting sites. The largest flocks are said to be made up of around five million individual birds. They are an awe-inspiring sight as the flock swoops and climbs creating ever changing shapes. From an observer's point of view the flock appears highly choreographed, but nothing can be further from the truth. Tens of thousands of individual birds are making individual decisions that lead to a magnificent dance.

These murmurations (so-called because of the sound of so many wings beating in unison) are not fully understood but are thought to form for mutual protection and possibly as a way of gathering in large numbers to keep each other warm at night. The intricate movements are created as each starling reacts to the movement of its six / seven closest neighbours.[5]

Think about that for a moment. A million individual birds making independent decisions appear to be choreographed. The explanation is that their independent decisions are influenced by the decisions being made by the other individuals around them. Multiply this effect out through a flock of five million birds and they appear to move as one and become capable of the awe-inspiring three-dimensional displays that can be seen in our autumn skies.

So it is with you and me. We are genuinely making independent decisions. We are not lying when we say to people: “no one can make the decision for you. The choice is yours.” But those choices are not free from influence. We are constantly reacting to the stimuli around us. We are part of a system. Our lives, our very identities, are shaped by the system and at the same time we contribute to shaping the system.

The creative benefits of multiple identities

Earlier we defined a healthy workplace community as one whose members have a shared identity. We also spoke of the danger that arises from communities becoming exclusive. In fact, we should seek out multiple communities, and develop multiple shared identities. It is by cultivating diverse connections that we unlock creativity.

According to Steven Johnson, "a good idea is a network",[6] and good ideas emerge from fluid networks. He shows how trade between the cities of northern Italy fuelled the Renaissance as ideas spilled over from one community to another.

> *"When the first market towns emerged in Italy, they didn't magically create some higher-level group consciousness. They simply widened the pool of minds that could come up with and share good ideas. This is not the wisdom of the crowd, but the wisdom of someone in the crowd. It's not that the network itself is smart; it's that the individuals get smarter because they're connected to the network."*[7]

In a closed community that isolates itself, the opportunity for creativity is limited and innovation is quickly replaced with group think. Where the magic happens is when each of us is connected to other communities. As ideas spill over from one community to the next they bump into new, adjacent ideas, and new possibilities emerge.

> *"All of us live inside our own private versions of the adjacent possible... we are surrounded by potential new configurations, new ways of breaking out of standard routines."[8]*
>
> Steven Johnson

When we all connect multiple communities, we turn our teams into nodes in the beautiful liquid network of humanity. They become the conduits that enable us to be inspired by others, and for us to provide inspiration for others.

The secret life of teams

Each of us is a unique human being. Biologically and psychologically, there is no one quite like you. When we create contexts in which we are willing both to see others for who they are and to turn up in such a way as to be seen, we create something very special.

We have seen the way in which the mycorrhizal network knits together the individual trees in a healthy forest. We heard Suzanne Simard describe how trees share resources, nurture immature plants, and communicate biochemical messages through the forest. Each individual tree playing its part in sustaining the forest.

Healthy workplace communities share many of the same characteristics. On the surface it appears that a set of individuals simply congregate to do a job of work. Below the surface the complex network of relationships transform them from a mere gathering of individuals into something bigger, something different. A living system in which difference and similarity drive constant adaptation. Where resources flow to where they are needed, and the team grows together. A human system in which each one of us has an essential role to play.

The concept of being an individual and being part of a system are not in competition with each other. As individuals we are made by the communities to which we belong ("I am because we are"). These communities uphold us, enable us, and give us everything we need to thrive. At the same time each of these communities need us to turn up with all our uniqueness, to value one another, and to share our resources. To work to enable the community to thrive is an act of loving others and, at the same time, it is to love ourselves.

With this in mind, the question becomes: how do we turn up for each other such that we and others in the community can flourish?

Try this thought experiment:

You add a unique ingredient to your team. No one is quite like you. Take some time to consider how you turn up, how you take your self to work.

What impact do your attitudes, words and behaviours have on the workplace community?

What would it mean for you to purposefully turn up in a way that enabled you and your colleagues to thrive?

Imagine you have worked in the same business for twenty years. Today is your leaving party. A string of people are going to get up and say a few words about what it has been like to have you in the community. What do you want them to say?

Now imagine you could listen in on the private conversations in that room. What would you want people to be saying about you? What difference do you want to have made to people and the business in those twenty years?

ENDNOTES

1 Dave Logan, John King, Halee Fischer-Wright, *Tribal leadership*, 2008, Harper Business, p.76-107

2 Dave Logan, John King, Halee Fischer-Wright, *Tribal leadership*, 2008, Harper Business, p.20-25

3 Ralph D Stacey etal., *Complexity and management*, 2002, Routledge, p.106

4 Ralph D Stacey etal., *Complexity and management*, 2002, Routledge, p.123

5 https://www.sciencefocus.com/nature/starling-murmurations/ (Accessed November 2025)

6 Steven Johnson, *Where good ideas come from*, 2010, Penguin, p.45

7 Steven Johnson, *Where good ideas come from*, 2010, Penguin, p.58

8 Steven Johnson, *Where good ideas come from*, 2010, Penguin, p.40

To see and be seen

"When people honour each other, there is a trust established that leads to synergy, interdependence, and deep respect."

Blaine Lee

We are social creatures. Our sense of self is formed and re-formed by our interactions with other people. Unsurprisingly then, our sense of purpose is formed as much from feeling appreciated as it is from the desire to make a difference.

A friend recently asked me about the "calling" I felt when I was at college. What was it exactly? The easy answer would have been to use spiritual terms, but it got me reflecting on the more human aspects. I realised it probably had three stages. The first was seeing someone else do the work and wanting to make the difference I could see that they were making. The second was a mentor who affirmed my ability to do the work, and the third was the wider confirmation that followed. So, if you strip away the intangible religious ideas like "God spoke to me" (I never claimed that) or "I just felt that God was calling me" (that doesn't even try to define the idea), what you have is two thirds about social interactions – I wanted to make the difference I saw someone else making, and others affirmed my belief that I was capable of doing it.

You will, occasionally come across people with such a strong desire to make a difference that they can plough a lonely furrow without the need for social affirmation. Most of us will not feel like our lives are purposeful unless that impact, or our potential to make that impact is acknowledged by others. Feeling valued is a powerful experience that shapes our thinking and our behaviours.

The power of recognition

In a ground breaking study of the motivations of employees Rachel Kranton and nobel prize winning economist George Akerlof demonstrated the extent to which we feel recognised has a direct impact on the way we turn up for work.[1] Their contribution to the developing field of behavioural economics was to introduce the concept of what they called "identity utility."

In economic terms, "utility" is defined as the total satisfaction or benefit derived from a certain state of the world. So, identity utility is the total satisfaction or benefit derived from an individual's sense of identity in any given situation. Conventional economics assumes that people make rational decisions (unaffected by emotion) that maximise their utility (satisfaction, happiness or welfare).[2] Behavioural economics challenged that approach and began to search for ways to describe how people actually make decisions.

What Kranton and Akerlof did was to introduce a way of describing how people's sense of identity shapes their decision making. What their work recognised was that each of us has a sense of who we are. We also have a sense of when our identity is being challenged, by our own behaviours and attitudes, or by those of others. When we are able to make choices that support or strengthen our sense of identity, we gain more satisfaction, and we feel happier (higher identity utility). When our choices undermine our sense of self, we experience a loss of satisfaction and feel less happy (lower identity utility). The attitudes, behaviours and expectations of others around us have the same effect.

When they tested their theory, Kranton and Akerlof found that when we identify with our work – when it feels like an expression of who we are – we enjoy higher levels of intrinsic reward (satisfaction, happiness, well-being). This internal reward is also enjoyed when we feel recognised and valued for who we are. When we enjoy this level of intrinsic reward, we are likely to place a lesser emphasis on the external rewards of salary, bonuses and benefits.

The reverse is also true. When we feel that our work does not fit with our sense of self; when we don't feel recognised or valued, we are likely to put a greater emphasis on external rewards. In economic terms, we seek compensation for our loss of identity utility (satisfaction, happiness and well-being).

To put it in terms with which we are now familiar – to get the most out of our working life we need be able to turn up as ourselves, and to feel recognised for who we are. We need our colleagues (especially our bosses) to see us, and we need to feel able to turn up in a way that makes our true selves seen.

Sawubona: I see you

Sikhona: I am here to be seen

Valuing the people around you

Up until now we have made an assumption that when others see us, they do so without prejudice or judgement. Certainly, the social contract contained in the greeting "Sawubona" and the related response "Sikhona" implies that we see each other for who we are and receive each other into the community in a non-judgemental and accepting way.

It's easier to put ourselves on the respondent's side of this contract. To be willing to be seen. It is more challenging to understand that we also need to be those who see others for who they are. With that role in this contract comes great responsibility. When we see others through lazy stereotypes and generalisations, we not only fail to see them, but we run the risk of doing them actual harm.

When I started my first business, a member of my family said, "People like us don't run businesses." It is a fascinating statement. Who are these "people like us?" For this relative "people like us" were "working folk" – employees not employers. In my relative's mind, we were strongly identified with a set of criteria; a set of norms; a set of limitations. People like us had an economic level it was foolish to seek to improve. We had a place in society that was subservient to others (even if grudgingly). We worked hard and we took home our pay cheque.

When I heard these words from my relative, I couldn't believe what I was hearing. At some level my upbringing has smashed through the barrier. I didn't recognise the attitude of my relative in my own life. That said, I recently realised how powerful that old belief had been in my childhood. I was talking with a friend about the story of Dick Whittington and his cat. As we talked, I realised that as a child I had understood the story as a moral tale about not getting above your station. In my mind the point of the story was that Dick Whittington had set off to find wealth in London, believing the streets to be "paved with gold", but instead had found hardship. It was only whilst talking with my friend I found myself remembering that Dick Whittington found wealth. The moral of the story was not that I should stay at home and not chase my dreams. It was that success is not found on streets paved with gold, but through hard work and determination. Subconsciously I had imbibed some of the same belief expressed by my relative and it had shaped the way I processed a story.

In her book *Mindset: the new psychology of success*, Carol Dweck explains how when we allow others to impose stereotypes onto us it can make us feel like we do not belong and, in turn, shape how we turn up. She describes a set of experiments that tried to understand the impact on people's work when the don't feel like they fit in.[3]

All the participants faced a measure of "othering" – negative stereotypes from others in the environment. Those students who were able to overcome this "othering" and grow saw the prejudice for what it was and interpreted it as reflecting poorly on those demonstrating that attitude. In their own minds they felt like they belonged, and they were able to turn up with confidence and grow.

Other participants were less able to overcome the othering, and the negative stereotypes were able to invade their sense of self. Over time their sense of belonging dwindled, their confidence waned, and ultimately, they removed themselves from the community. Two conclusions emerge from this story:

1. When we feel comfortable with ourselves it equips us to fight back against unhelpful stereotypes. We don't have to be what others believe us to be. Their limitations are not ours. I am who I am and I am not defined by the way others describe me.
2. When we are interacting with the people around us, we wield great power. And, as Peter Parker (Spider-Man) was reminded, "with great power, comes great responsibility". That responsibility is the responsibility to see people for who they are, not for who we think they are, or who we think they should be. It is a responsibility to see in everyone their unique and amazing potential. Not someone we know because we know "people like them" but someone we have never met before, whom we can get to know.

We all want to be valued for who we are and the only way that can happen is if we all value others for who they are. When people feel recognised and valued, they feel like they belong. It is when we feel like we belong, that we also feel free to develop our own distinctiveness.

When we feel valued, we find our work more satisfying, more enjoyable, more fulfilling, and as a result, become more committed, more productive and more effective in our work. When we feel valued it has a positive impact on our mental health, our physical health, our relationships, our productivity and our general outlook. Life is better when we value each other.

Try this thought experiment:

Taking your self to work is a choice to turn up in a way that you can be seen and to see, and value other people for who they are.

Think about the people you work with.

- How well do you know them?
- What do you believe about your colleagues?
- What are those beliefs based on?

The only way to avoid lazy stereotypes, is to make a conscious decision to get to know people for who they are. What will you do this week to put aside any preconceived ideas about people and to really get to know them?

ENDNOTES

1 George A Akerlof and Rachel E Kranton, *Identity economics*, 2010, Princeton University Press

2 Morris Altman, *Behavioral economics for dummies*, 2012, Wiley and Sons, p.108

3 Carol S. Dweck, *Mindset: the new psychology of success*, 2006, Ballantine Books, p.77-78

To see is to be grateful

"I would maintain that thanks are the highest form of thought, and that gratitude is happiness doubled by wonder."

G.K. Chesterton

As businesses in the UK began to emerge from the restrictions of Covid 19, a client asked me what we could do to help reconnect their employees with each other. As with many businesses, the impact of working restrictions had been different on different employees. Some had been furloughed, some had worked from home, some had worked in a hybrid model and others were required on the ground with all the requirements for PPE and social distancing. Returning to work, my client observed that the teams had lost cohesion. They had come to see each other as competitors. They had lost sight of the interdependence that made the business work.

We chatted about what the client was seeing, about behaviours and dialogue, and out of it emerged a question: what could we do to encourage people to appreciate each other more?

What followed for me was a chain of thinking that began with exploring the nature and power of gratitude, pulled together thinking I had done over the previous 10 years, and ultimately led to me writing this book.

Gratitude pulls together the two parts of the greeting we have considered.

Sawubona [I see you]
Sikhona [I am here to be seen]

Gratitude is about seeing others, and it is a choice we make as to how we ourselves turn up. To practice gratitude is to choose to make a positive difference to those around us and it is to value the positive difference they make to us.

What is gratitude?

When I speak about gratitude in businesses, I invariably get the same initial response. Suspecting they are about to get a shallow motivational talk about saying thank you, people frown and jump in with reasons why saying "thank you" for everything can be cheesy and meaningless. Some would even say downright annoying.

The critics are right – words without meaning are just noise. To hear someone say "thank you" when their attitude betrays their lack of appreciation is probably more detrimental than if nothing were said. On the other hand, we can communicate our appreciation without necessarily saying "thank you".

There are two sides to gratitude:[1]

- Appreciating the value of things
- Recognising the source of goodness

The first of these does not involve any external expression. In the words of Robert Emmons "gratitude is an affirmation of goodness."[2] It is the ability to look at life and to notice the good things and, in noticing, to take stock and to value them.

Sounds simple, doesn't it? The trouble is that our brains are wired in ways that prevent us from noticing the good things, and when we do, to stop us appreciating them. The problem is that our brains are bombarded with more data than we can possibly process, and they are constantly choosing what to notice and what to simply ignore. Anything that is "normal" or "to be expected" is likely to pass unnoticed. Instead, the brain seeks out novelty and quickly gets used to the normal. That way we learn to cope with persistent challenges, but we also quickly take for granted the day-to-day good things in our lives.

Without meaning to, we become ungrateful for the things we have. This is the foundation on which consumerism is born. As someone once pointed out: remember everything you have was once something you wanted.

As one of the world's leading experts on the psychology of gratitude, Robert Emmons identifies eight obstacles to gratitude.[3] Among these are what he calls "negativity bias". This is the survival mechanism by which our brains are poised to react negatively whenever anything significant happens in our environment. It is a survival mechanism that creates caution and prepares us for a quick withdrawal. The downside is that it creates a psychological focus on the negative aspects of life. In a context in which we rarely have to run for our lives, we easily resort to complaints and resentments.

Interestingly one of the other obstacles to gratitude identified by Emmons relates to aspects of life that we have had cause to notice in the progress of this book. That is, our unwillingness to acknowledge our dependence on others. The value our modern society often places on the illusion of self-sufficiency prevents us from appreciating the value brought into our lives by others.

This is the importance of the time we spent considering the interdependence of life. Once we see it, once we shed old beliefs about self-sufficiency, we open ourselves up to benefit from the people around us, and we open ourselves up to gratitude.

When we are working in a team that is functioning well, stuff is done on time, data flows to where it needs to go and arrives in a timely way, and everyone contributes their bit to the corporate jigsaw. We get used to it. We stop noticing. We stop acknowledging other people's contribution. We start to feel undervalued by the people around us.

That brings us to the second side to gratitude: recognising the source of the good things that are part of our lives. Recognising the little things that make our lives better is only half the journey, and some people get stuck there. They derive a sense of personal greatness from the richness of their lives. "Look at the variety of experiences with which I fill my life!" "Look at the spiritual insight I have!" "Look at my amazing home!" I'm sure you could continue that list of examples, and you recognise the subtext – "aren't I amazing." There are even versions of this that use the language of gratitude, but which ultimately translate as: "I am so grateful for how wonderful I am." To think like this is to put ourselves in the centre of life and to be caught up in the myth of the "self-made man".

The thing is, we are all in danger of occupying this self-centred space, and that danger arises from becoming so used to the value others add to our lives that we stop seeing them. It's how our brains are wired, and we need to deliberately create moments of mindfulness that bring our attention back to recognising the source of goodness.

This needn't be time-consuming or onerous. It can be simple disciplines. I remember a conversation in a workshop in which one of the participants recognised how self-centred their approach to work had become. They spoke of how this led to impatience with others. They recognised that, without realising it, they had learned to behave as if everyone else was simply there for them. The solution they came up with was simple. In front of their colleagues, they made the commitment that, when they needed to speak with someone, they would take a ten-second pause to notice how busy everyone else was. Being mindful of this simple fact was enough to adjust their mindset, to value the work their colleagues did, and to value any time their colleagues took away from their main task to support them.

Recognising the source of goodness requires the commitment implied by the greeting: “Sawubona” [I see you]. Earlier we spoke of that greeting as a social contract. An agreement that sits at the heart of healthy communities – to see others – and to turn up so that we can be seen. When we make that commitment to each other, we commit to live with our eyes open to the richness others bring into our lives.

A useful tool from the world of process improvement

As I chatted with my client about ways in which we could encourage people to appreciate each other we realised that what we were really talking about was highlighting the humanity at the heart of the business’s processes. The simple recognition that in a business we work interdependently. We can’t function without receiving what we need from others, and everything we do has a direct impact on the ability others have to do their work. To put it in the terms used by process engineers: for everything I do, I have suppliers and customers.

In the world of process mapping, they capture this idea in a SIPOC chart.

Supplier	Input	Process	Output	Customer

To fill in this chart you start in the middle by identifying the process you want to focus on. From there you can identify all the "inputs" required for the process to function. Once the inputs are identified you can identify the "supplier" of each input. On the right side of the chart you can identify all the outputs from the process and the "customer(s)" for each output.

You may be glad to know that we are not about to dive into the world of process engineering. The takeaway is much more basic; it is simply to recognise the principle that we can only function because of our "suppliers" and everything we do creates a set of "outputs" that affects our "customers".

It's probably easier to think about this in the context of the work you do. Isolate any task and ask yourself what do you need to do that work? You may need equipment, bits of information or physical parts. For each of these ask yourself, where does that come from? Who is responsible for making sure my equipment works? Who is responsible for supplying the information I need? Who is responsible for making sure the parts I need are available? These are your suppliers and – here's the thing – your job would be impossible without them.

Most of the time, everything you need will just be there. Your computer will be on your desk, there will be pens, copies of forms, a printer, a telephone. When you log onto your computer the information you need will be there for you. The day passes and you may not even think about the work other people have done to make your work possible. You've had a good day – everything went smoothly – and your brain pays no attention to the fact that the hidden work of others made your good day possible.

Then you have a day when your computer doesn't work, and the IT person is tied up in meetings. Or you log onto your computer to find a vital document has not been uploaded. You feel the stress; you notice your suppliers have not supplied you with what you need. You spend the day on the phone chasing stuff from other people. It's a bad day and you know who caused it.

It's back to how our brains are wired to ignore the normal and spot the abnormal, to take for granted the good stuff and to notice the threats.

Take a moment now to notice the stuff you don't normally notice. Allow yourself to recognise the people whose work makes your work possible. Notice that you are part of a system without which you couldn't function. Identify specific people who enable your work and allow yourself to recognise the value they add to your work and to your experience of work.

Finally take time to recognise that your work supplies other people. The way you work has a direct impact on others. Your attitudes and behaviours at work directly shape their experience of work. Every day you are the difference between a good day and a bad day for other people around you. Every day you contribute, for better or worse, to the well-being and mental health of those around you.

The process of life

Whilst the principle of SIPOC is easier to illustrate in the context of work, it is probably even more relevant in life. Earlier in the book we had cause to notice the network of people behind our grocery shopping. Imagine how big that network of suppliers becomes when you take in every other element of your life. Now expand it further as you consider those whose input into your life is less practical but social and emotional. Far from being independent islands we are deeply embedded in a system without which we could not survive.

When you notice this, take time again to consider the inputs that make your life possible. Notice the way so many strangers, whose names you will never know, contribute to your well-being, make good days possible and provide support on more challenging days. Notice the inputs from friends and family, and from your wider social network.

Finally take time to notice how you have inputs into the lives of others around you. What you do, the way you choose to speak and behave directly shapes the way the people around you experience life. Every day you are the difference between a good day and a bad day for other people around you. Every day you contribute, for better or worse, to the well-being and mental health of those around you.

Allow yourself to be grateful for your suppliers, and make a decision to be a positive difference to the lives of your customers.

Keeping it real (sometimes gratitude isn't warranted)

Wouldn't this world be an amazing place to live if every input anyone made into the life of another was positive? Sadly, we all know that is not the case. If we are honest, we know that, at times, all of us are responsible for those negative inputs. We can resolve to have a positive impact on everyone we meet but, in this, as in everything else, perfection is beyond us.

There is a version of the gratitude mindset promoted by the shallow gurus of the feel-good lifestyle that says: there is something to be grateful for in everything. Pushed hard this idea becomes toxic. Is the victim of abuse to feel grateful for their abuse? Is the starving family grateful towards those who use starvation as a weapon in their territorial war? Too many people have been damaged by the idea that we should find the good in everything. The danger being threefold:

1. The felt pressure to downplay situations and people that have a negative / destructive impact on our lives.

2. The self-criticism for negative feelings – when they are understandable and justified.
3. The loss of impetus to remove yourself from a situation.

There will always be things you can be grateful for, but you don't need to be grateful for everything.

Amie Gordon warns of four other ways in which giving thanks can backfire:[4]

- Overdosing on gratitude: It is the quality of gratitude rather than the quantity that counts. Avoid expressions of gratitude becoming frivolous and meaningless. "In a study of gratitude journaling, people who tracked their gratitude once per week were happier after six weeks than when they began, whereas those who tracked their gratitude three times per week were not."[5]
- Papering over the cracks: Gratitude is great at building a positive culture but don't use it to avoid serious problems. "In fact, when it comes to serious problems, a negative emotion like anger may actually be more constructive. In one study of romantic couples, expressing anger was more beneficial than being positive, when discussing a severe problem, because the anger helped couples address and resolve the issue rather than sweep it under the rug."[6]

- Downplaying your own success: recognising our interdependence doesn't preclude recognising personal success. We may not be able to achieve anything without the support of the system but with the support of the system we can all experience success. We should own and celebrate that success.
- Mistaking gratitude for indebtedness: Being grateful does not imply indebtedness. Gratitude recognises that we all receive benefits from others. When your colleagues do their job well it makes your life better. You benefit, hopefully you reciprocate by doing your job to the best of your ability, but you are not in each other's debt. Gratitude acknowledges the goodness or value received in the flow of life. Indebtedness treats that goodness as a transaction – a supply for which payment is due. When the shopkeeper hands over their produce, payment is due. When the shopkeeper treats me kindly and makes me smile, I feel grateful.

To practice gratitude is not only to value and appreciate the good things that come to us in life but in expressing our gratitude we choose to have a positive impact on those around us. We choose to see them, to value them and to let them know that they are valued.

When we turn up for each other, when we recognise our interdependence, and when we value the richness others bring to our lives, we create a community in which we can all thrive.

Try this thought experiment:

Put together your own SIPOC chart of the "Process of Life." You can be as high level or as granular as you want (maybe start off at a high level).

Start with the question:

- What do I do that adds value to my life (the process)?

Then ask:

- What do I need in order to be able to do this activity (the inputs)?
- Who supplies what I need (the suppliers)?

Now you have identified your suppliers take time to acknowledge the value they add to your life.

You may also want to look at the impact your activity has on others. What does your activity produce (outputs) and who benefits (clients)?

ENDNOTES

1 Robert Emmons with Jeremy Adam Smith, *The gratitude project*, 2020, New Harbinger Publications, p.6

2 Robert Emmons with Jeremy Adam Smith, *The gratitude project*, 2020, New Harbinger Publications, p.6

3 Robert A. Emmons, *Thanks!: How practicing gratitude can make you happier*, 2008, Houghton and Mifflin, p.127-140

4 Amie Gordon: *Five ways giving thanks can backfire*, in Jeremy Adam Smith, *The gratitude project*, 2020, New Harbinger Publications, p.84-85

5 Amie Gordon: *Five ways giving thanks can backfire*, in Jeremy Adam Smith, *The gratitude project*, 2020, New Harbinger Publications, p.84

6 Amie Gordon: *Five ways giving thanks can backfire*, in Jeremy Adam Smith, *The gratitude project*, 2020, New Harbinger Publications, p.85

Part four:
Turning up to be the difference

Express your self – mission and purpose

Your life is what it is because of the goodness you experience from a multitude of other people. The people with whom you work are an interdependent community of people working together to achieve the objectives of the business. They need you to turn up in a way that you can be seen. They need you to turn up with a willingness to see, and value, them for who they are. When you do that, you are in a position to be deliberate in the difference you choose to make. You can identify your purpose.

We all know how easy it is to get sucked into living for something that is not yet here. It may be a big family event like a wedding. It could be the ticket to see your favourite band perform live, or the holiday of a lifetime planned for next summer. These things naturally draw our attention, but in focusing on these future events it is all too easy to miss out on the riches of each day.

> *"Perfection of character is this: to live each day as if it were your last, without frenzy, without apathy, without pretence."* [1]
>
> Marcus Aurelius

To some, the idea of living every day as if it were your last, seems morbid. After all, we live in an era in which philosophers are contemplating what they call "escape velocity": the theory that, in the not-too-distant future, medical science will reach a point at which it is outpacing the causes of death. Such philosophers rejoice in the dream of a healthy immortal life. In such a context the suggestion by philosophers like Marcus Aurelius that we should live in the knowledge of our mortality seems pessimistic.

To see it this way is to miss the point. Those philosophers who call on us to maintain an awareness of our mortality do so with the view that it is the inevitable arrival of death that gives life meaning. It is the dark contrast to the light of every new day. It is the reason not to put off until tomorrow what you can do today. It is freedom to throw off pretence and to be true to yourself.

By all means, plan for tomorrow, but live for today.

You are here for a reason (or are you?)

I find it fascinating when I hear non-religious people use phrases like: "this is what I was put here to do," or "I feel like I was put on this earth to do this." I want to ask them who they think put them here, but that would seem churlish. What is clear is that, even to those who don't believe in a higher power, the idea of receiving a "calling" remains a powerful concept in our post-religious culture and it is fraught with danger.

Mission and purpose are buzzwords in both business and life. Many writers and speakers have expressed an imperative to discover your "purpose" if you want to live meaningfully. This has led many people into a frustrating search for a purpose that is external to themselves. The most obvious questions being: "where is it going to come from?" and "how will you know it is the real thing?"

I remember in my thirties having a conversation that began to open up a much more helpful approach to the idea of mission and purpose. I was still working in the church and was chatting with an older, more experienced colleague. We were talking about the "calling to the ministry" – the idea that God directly calls individuals to the task. My colleague expressed a view that took me by surprise and is probably still rare in the church. "It's a load of rubbish! There is no such thing as a calling from God! If you have the ability, then you have a duty to use it and that is all there is. God does not speak directly to individuals to 'call' them."

I was shocked, but the conversation stayed with me and planted the seed of questions that I think apply to anyone (religious or not) who feels the need for an external calling.

- What exactly are you looking for?
- How will you recognise it when it arrives?
- How will you verify it is real and not imagined?
- [If you don't have a specific faith] Who or what is determining your purpose?

Even whilst still considering myself a Christian I began to question the idea of a specific calling. I would meet people who said they felt God was calling them to a specific work. What was I to do? How was this calling to be verified? I remember a complete stranger arriving in our congregation and within weeks telling me he was called to youth work. When, in the interest of protecting our young people, I declined to give him a role he accused me of denying him his divine service. If you believe in an inner calling from God, then his complaint had a logic to it. How can another human being question an inner calling? This gentleman was not the only one with whom I had this type of conversation.

If you think you have been put on the earth for a specific purpose, or to achieve a specific mission it is a huge boost to the ego. The challenge comes when you find yourself no longer able to fulfil that purpose or mission. When the sense of calling is replaced with silence, and a complete lack of external direction. Redundancy, serious illness or injury are among the many circumstances of life that can suddenly challenge a sense of calling.

When I chose to step away from my calling, I felt lost. I previously mentioned a significant phone call in which a friend had said:

"Ian, you need to realise that you are not who you are because you were a minister. You were a minister because of who you are."

That statement unlocked a lot of things for me. Among the things it unlocked was the door to the prison I had created for myself with my sense of calling. If my work in the church had flowed out of who I was, then I simply needed to find other contexts in which I could express the things that were important to me. My purpose does not define me. I define my purpose. My purpose is to live out my values in a way that is true to myself. I had done so for nearly two decades in the church community. Now I could go on and find other communities in which to express myself.

If you have a religious faith, then you may feel that your god(s) or the universe have put you here for a reason; that there is some external authority working out its plan through you. If you are not religious, then you may just feel you are here by accident. Either way the best way to understand where you can make a positive difference is not to look for a sign, or a voice that calls you, but to understand yourself. To recognise what you bring to the world – your values, your personality, your abilities, your resources, your time and your compassion – and to find places where you can make a positive difference to the world whilst you are here.

Ikigai

The Japanese word *ikigai* translates as "reason to live" and has come to encapsulate a concept of purposeful living that is thought to originate on the island of Okinawa. This prefecture of Japan is famous for the longevity and good health of its population. Many of these elderly people are said to attribute their well-being to their strong sense of *ikigai*.

One of the earliest uses of the word *ikigai* appears to be in the fourteenth century epic *The Tale of the Heike* that tells the story of the samurai clans who clashed in the Genpai war (1180–1185). There we find the words: "having purpose in life [ikigai] gives one a strong will to live."

In the twentieth century the word came to represent a model that describes the ingredients that come together to define an individual's unique *ikigai*. These ingredients are:

1. What you love
2. What the world needs
3. What you are good at
4. What you can be paid for

At the intersection of what you love and what you are good at is passion. When what you love intersects with what the world needs you have a mission. When the world is prepared to pay you to meet its needs you have a vocation. And where the world is prepared to pay you for what you are good at, you have a profession.

The definitions of mission and vocation are noteworthy. Mission is defined not by what I feel I want to do (or am called to do) but by the needs of others. Similarly, vocation is defined not by "calling" but by the much more objective idea of being paid to meet a need.

Perhaps most significant in the context of our journey is that the concept *ikigai* grows out of self-awareness. Discovering your "reason to live" is a process that starts with self-discovery, and from a place of self-awareness asks, 'What does the world need that I can provide?'

One purpose and many missions

"Purpose isn't a cause; it is an approach to work and serving others. Purpose is a verb, not a noun." [2]

Aaron Hurst

In the early years following my career change, I longed for a new cause and a new sense of purpose. I needed someone to help me reframe my understanding of living purposefully. At this point I owe a huge debt to Aaron Hurst whose book *The Purpose Economy* enabled me to move forward. In the book, Hurst makes a distinction between "purpose" and "cause". He defines purpose as an approach shaped by "who we are and what matters to us personally"[3] On the other hand, he defines a "cause" as a singular expression of purpose. If purpose is about finding direction, causes are the destinations along the way.

My mind tends to process this distinction better as being between purpose and missions, but it is the same idea. Your purpose is about how you approach the work of serving others. It finds expression in a multitude of contexts – family, community, work and society. In these contexts, you may identify specific missions – defined opportunities to make a specific difference. During your life, missions will come and go. Over time, missions also change in their nature. The difference I can make now for my adult children is not the same as it was when they were young, and in years to come (should I live long enough) the difference I will make to them when my capacity is limited will be different again.

Your impact network

Once we embrace the idea that our purpose is an approach to life that will express itself in multiple missions then we can simplify our search for purpose. By pulling together some of the thinking we have done in previous chapters we can identify the ingredients of our own purpose:

- Recognising that we are part of a human system that is bigger than any of us as individuals.
- Making a choice to serve that system – to make a positive difference.
- Understanding what matters to us personally.
- Understanding the kind of difference we can make by turning up in a genuine way.

Here is where we need to put the work in. It is not enough to say: "my purpose is to make a difference by being me." What does "being me" mean in that sentence?

You won't find the answer by looking inwards. You'll find it by looking outwards. Your purpose is out there at the interface between your self and the world of which you are a part.

One way of doing that is to simply consider what I describe as your impact network. The theory here is that every connection is an opportunity to make a positive difference. Remember, making a difference isn't a choice. The choice is what kind of difference will you make?

Your impact network falls into three categories:

– **Family and friends**

– **Workplace contacts**

– **Society** (Neighbours, charities, voluntary work, etc.)

If your mission is an expression of who you are, what is important to you and the difference you want to make then the questions become:

- What is important to me in this context?
- What is the need that I can meet?
- What difference do I want to make?
- How do I need to turn up to have this impact?

Maybe it is even as simple as asking, in each of these contexts, what would it mean to turn up to see and be seen?

If we are to understand what it means for us to be the difference in each of these contexts, then it is probably helpful to break these networks down.

Charity begins at home

In 1642, Sir Thomas Browne coined the phrase "charity begins at home". What he had in mind was not what we would call charitable giving, but something much more profound.

If you have attended a wedding at a very traditional church, you may have heard the version from the King James Bible, dating back to 1608:

> *Charity suffereth long, and is kind; charity envieth not; charity vaunteth not itself, is not puffed up, Doth not behave itself unseemly, seeketh not her own, is not easily provoked, thinketh no evil; Rejoiceth not in iniquity, but rejoiceth in the truth; Beareth all things, believeth all things, hopeth all things, endureth all things. Charity never faileth*[4]

The word being translated as "charity" is the Greek word "agapé" which is understood to be self-sacrificing love that is committed to the well-being of others.

This was the kind of "charity" Thomas Browne had in mind. The idea that "Charity begins at home" is the idea that love ripples out from its centre touching those closest to us first. There is no sense that love is a finite resource that may not be capable of expanding beyond the home, or that there are those beyond its reach. The sense is rather that love should be felt first by those closest to us, and that the home is where we learn to love others. A functional home is where we learn to look outside of ourselves, beyond our own needs and desires, and develop a concern for the well-being of others.

You could conceive of your impact network as acknowledging those radiating circles of love. Closest to the centre are your family and friends, then come your workplace colleagues and finally the rest of society.

Before moving on to consider how your purpose finds expression at home, we should probably acknowledge what may feel like a huge leap in our thinking. From talking about purpose and making a difference, I have suddenly introduced the idea of love. Actually, it is not the first time we have used the word. We have already established that self-love is at the heart of healthy communities. Now we are taking that thinking one step further: the missions through which we express our purpose are acts of love.

In the systems view of life that we have explored, the delineation between self-love and love for others is blurred. Given that we benefit from the well-being of the system, every act of love towards another person is an act of self-love. In seeking the well-being of others, we enrich the system that nurtures us. Ubuntu: I am because we are.

Being the difference for family and friends

Those closest to us are, in the same moment, most important to our own well-being and most likely to be taken for granted. I am not going to attempt to re-write the volumes that have been written about how to nurture healthy relationships with friends and family. I am simply going to point out that, among those we feel most able to be ourselves, we still need to be deliberate in the way we turn up.

In business, they often say that if you fail to plan then you are planning to fail. Among our family and friends, we need to be deliberate about making a positive difference.

- What difference do you want to make to your partner / parents / children/ brothers / sisters / friends?
- What needs do they have that you could meet?
- What is the difference you want to make in their lives?
- How do you need to turn up to have this impact.

If you can answer these questions, then you can summarise them into a mission statement (or a set of mission statements). Each would read something like this:

"My mission as a [insert relationship] is to __________, by being __________."

Remember, this is not about being something you are not. It is about understanding yourself and identifying how you can turn up so that you are the difference they need you to be.

Being the difference for your workplace contacts

In many ways the considerations here are exactly the same as those in your family. It's about how you turn up in your workplace relationships such that you have a positive impact on the well-being of others. It is the same set of questions:

- What difference do you want to make to your colleagues / suppliers / customers?
- What needs do they have that you could meet?
- What is the difference you want to make in their lives?
- How do you need to turn up to have this impact.

At work, a new consideration comes into play: you have a specific role in the community, a set of predefined responsibilities, a set of business objectives to fulfil.

- Given your role, what difference do you want to make?
- What needs could you, in your specific role, meet?
- How can you use your role to make a difference in the lives of those around you?
- How do you need to turn up in your role to have this impact?

Being the difference to society

When we come to this biggest of contexts, we have to acknowledge that some of us can get overwhelmed by the scale of the opportunity / challenge. How can I ("little me") make a difference?

So, here it is probably most helpful to go back to the thought that just by being part of the system we make a difference. From the contagion of a smile, to the concept of "pass it forward", our attitudes, behaviours and actions act as an endless stream of pebbles thrown into the proverbial pond – rippling outwards.

Some people change the world one relationship at a time.

For most of us, the most accessible way to make a difference to society is through being part of organisations that make a difference. In this way, we leverage the power of community. In an organisation seeking to change the world, I don't have to change the world, I just have to contribute my skills, my time and my insight to a system. Alone I might not be able to change the world, but together we can.

Identifying your workplace missions

Engaging meaningfully with our work is about understanding the different ways in which our purpose can express itself in the context of our workplace community. What impact can we have? Where does the organisation in which we work present opportunities for us to express our purpose? Where are the opportunities to be ourselves and to make a difference to the things that matter to us?

I would suggest there are three kinds of mission that can be found in the context of our work:

- **Big picture missions**
- **Role based missions**
- **Relational missions**

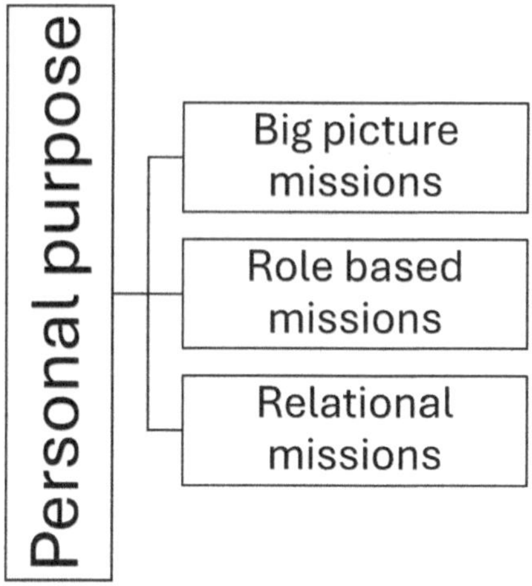

Big picture missions

You will find the possibility for a "big picture" mission where you have an opportunity to work for an organisation whose purpose aligns with your own sense of purpose.

In a big picture mission, your role within the organisation may not be particularly inspiring for you, but the idea that every day you will be contributing to the organisational purpose is. Think of the proverbial cleaner at NASA who, when asked what he was doing, replied, "I'm helping to put a man on the moon."

Role-based missions

Imagine you are a HR professional who is deeply motivated by creating workplace environments in which people can thrive. The big picture purpose of the organisation is not inspiring to you, but the company has a reputation for actively promoting policies and activities that improve the experience and well-being of their employees. You may not feel personal commitment to the purpose for which the organisation exists but the role that is open to you creates a great context in which you can do your thing.

Relational missions

This last level could be said to exist in almost every workplace. Identifying your mission at this level is about choosing to make a difference to the people whose lives intersect with your own. The specifics of your role or even the organisation in which you work are irrelevant to this level of mission.

Finding purpose at work is not necessarily about looking for an organisation whose reason for existence aligns perfectly with your own. It is about identifying the potential to express your own sense of purpose.

Be you and make the difference

Having briefly explored the kinds of mission that are out there for you to adopt, I want to bring this back to the thought that underpins this entire chapter.

Purpose is found in understanding who you are and what matters to you. It's not hard. You don't need the universe to show you what it needs. Be who you are. Turn up with a deliberate intention to make a positive impact at every level.

Be yourself, and in being yourself make a positive difference to those around you – in your family, at work and in wider society.

Be you and make a difference.

Try this thought experiment:

Take time to reflect on your personal missions across different areas of your impact network (Family and friends – Workplace contacts – Society). For each area, answer the four questions below and complete at least one mission statement.

1. What is important to me in this context?
2. What is the need I can meet?
3. What difference do I want to make?
4. How do I need to turn up to have this impact?

Use the following format for each mission statement

My mission as a [insert relationship] is to ________, by being ________.

ENDNOTES

1 Marcus Aurelius, *Meditations*, 2006, Penguin, p.69
2 Aaron Hurst, *The purpose economy*, 2014, Elevate, p.101
3 Aaron Hurst, *The purpose economy*, 2014, Elevate, p.108
4 1 Corinthians 13:4-9, King James Version

Turning up for each other

This is our moment to turn up and be the difference. One moment, one choice, one connection at a time.

You play an essential role

We may occasionally think of someone we work with as irreplaceable. You may even have had the honour of being described that way yourself. It is a wonderful compliment, and our egos certainly enjoy the idea. But is it ever true? In a healthy business and in other social contexts, the truth is that life will go on without us. Recognising this removes a burden from us. To believe you are indispensable creates a sense of responsibility that is too heavy for anyone to carry.

A colleague of mine reflected on how people who are removed from the workplace for an extended time are sometimes enabled to realise that there is more to life than work. They return to businesses and teams that have continued without them. Sometimes even to clients who now prefer to work with the person who filled the gap. They can slot back into fulfilling an essential role, but they now understand that they are replaceable, and that knowledge gives them permission to switch off and to give attention to other parts of their lives.

At the other end of the spectrum, it is possible to look at the vastness of the universe and to consider ourselves irrelevant specks that, in the vastness of time, exist for a moment and are gone. Surely then, the ideas we have played with are the arrogant, egocentric ideas of a species that has become too big for its boots. Surely, looked at in this way, our species, let alone each of us as an individual, is an irrelevance. In the exploration that follows we'll see that this too is untrue.

Here is the thing: it is possible to be essential without being irreplaceable. You have an essential – if finite – role to play. For the time you are here, we need you to be you.

A brief visit to the world of neuroplasticity

Our brains are remarkable biological machines and the more we understand about them the more remarkable we realise they are. Neuro-imaging techniques allow scientists to measure brain activity and to observe the communication between specific neurons in real time. In doing this they can identify specific neural pathways used by the brain for specific functions. Each neuron in those pathways is performing an essential role.

It is when these techniques are used to monitor brain activity in people who have suffered brain injury that we see how truly amazing the brain is. We now know that when the brain is damaged it can adapt and essentially rewire itself to fulfil the functions previously served by the damaged tissue. The neurons that had been serving an essential function, but which were destroyed by the injury, are replaced. The brain finds new ways of continuing without them.

It is possible to play an essential role within a system without being irreplaceable. Like the individual neurons in the neural pathways of a brain, we are each playing an essential role in the world, in society, in our communities, workplaces and families. When something happens that finally removes us from the "system", the system will adapt and find another way to continue. Until then we need you. We need each other. Each one of us is playing an essential role.

"I am, because we are." Each of us contributes to the system, and together we achieve more than we could ever achieve as a collection of individuals.

The choice

Remember the observer principle? The concept from particle physics that suggests it is impossible to stand outside the system. Even if you see yourself as marginal or have made a choice to keep your head down and just do what you are paid to do, you are making a difference to the organisation you work for and the lives of the people around you.

Cast your mind back to high school chemistry lessons. At some point your teacher introduced you to the inert, or noble, gases. These elements do not readily react with other elements. Think of them as the people in your organisation who keep themselves to themselves, who don't tend to speak up – they just get on with their work.

But here is the thing: inert gases make a difference. They are used to prevent unwanted chemical reactions. They prevent bacteria growing on packaged food. They prevent oil tankers from blowing up. They make a big difference.

I'm not suggesting that you should seek to be inert, shrink into your shell and stay out of the way. I think you'll find that, by doing so, you are more likely to be the cause of a negative reaction. The point I'm making is simpler than that; it is that you need to embrace the fact that you will make a difference.

Your choice is what kind of difference do you want to make?

Being the difference

The primary way you make a difference at work is by being you. Turning up as yourself doesn't mean turning up with all of you on display at once. The choice to make a positive difference in the way you turn up at work is about choosing which aspects of you will be most appropriate, most effective. Which parts of you will enable you to be the difference you want to be.

We all have the potential to be decisive problem-solvers and we all have the potential to be more contemplative listeners. True, we may have a natural tendency towards one or the other, but we can make the choice.

One family story that occasionally gets dusted off in our family is how I impressed my future in-laws by the way I handled my car breaking down. It was my first visit to their home, and my first meeting with my wife's parents. I was twenty and we had driven up to Yorkshire in my old 1978 VW Polo that had 90,000 miles on the clock (impressive for an engine built in the '70s).

If you knew me you would know that my preference is to be the more reflective, slow and steady person who wants to make sure that everyone is OK. The flip side of that, of course, is that I can be indecisive.

So here I am outside the home of my future in-laws, and my car won't start. Without thinking, I went into action and quickly got the breakdown service out. There was no fuss, no dithering just decisive action. The story is that some years later my father-in-law said that the way I handled the incident allayed worries that I was a bit too young to be in a relationship with his daughter (my wife is older than me).

What I see in that story is that, when it is appropriate I am capable of being a decisive problem-solver and I shouldn't let my preference for being slower and more reflective stop me from backing myself when something more direct is required.

To be more self-critical, when I turn up in a way that allows my preferred way of working to get in the way, I essentially make a choice (even if subconscious) to turn up in an unhelpful way. In effect I choose not to be a positive difference.

There is a useful exercise I picked up from my colleague Myles Downey. He suggests that at the beginning of the day take a look at your diary and identify two or three personal attributes that would be useful in enabling you to do what you need to do well. Write them down and, on a scale of 1–10, score yourself on how much of that attribute you feel is present at the beginning of the day. Repeat the exercise at lunchtime and finally score yourself at the end of the day. You will often find that simply doing this exercise shifts something in your subconscious that brings those attributes to the fore and your scores will rise through the day.

The little things that make a difference

I remember working with a medium-sized business who wanted to promote mutual appreciation across their 160 employees. Over the course of a number of days everyone participated in a short workshop. We got people talking about what would make them feel valued and what they could do to communicate how much they valued their colleagues. What stood out to me was that it was the little things that made the biggest difference. Things like remembering people's names or not assuming that what you want has priority in someone else's day.

When it comes to choosing to be the difference it will be the little things that have the biggest impact. It will be the way you manage your own behaviour. The tone of your conversation. Your choice as to whether to have a bit of a moan, or to look for the positive in a situation.

I'm not talking here about having a permanent fake grin or bouncing up to the person who is having a bad day and telling them to cheer up. Neither of those things will make a positive difference. We all have bad days, and we'll all have days where we don't show up in the best way possible. Rather, I'm back to the need to be self-aware. Being aware of the impact you are having on others and being deliberate about it. Being aware that your attitude, your choice of words, your mood affects those around you.

Here is the wonder of group dynamics. When you are struggling others will be doing OK and will be able to support you. When you are having a great day, others will be struggling, and you will be able to support them.

Growing together

In my early to mid-teens I played squash to a decent level. My fondest memories are from a period in which I only ever really played one other person. We were well matched in our ability, and we were both incredibly competitive on the court. My game came on in leaps and bounds. I was enjoying myself, I was being challenged and I felt recognised.

The challenge of this book has been to turn up for each other. To turn up as yourself. To turn up with the intent to make a positive difference to the lives of others. And, to value the benefits that flow into your life when others turn up in your life.

In this kind of environment, we will create for each other the perfect ground in which to put down roots, and to grow together. We described healthy workplace communities as places where people experienced psychological safety. When people feel safe, they are enabled to float ideas, to talk openly, to challenge one another. All ingredients needed for growth.

I have a dream: A working life well lived

Behind this book is a dream of an ideal world, a world in which human beings understand their interdependent relationship with one another and the world in which we live. A world where everyone is valued and everyone can flourish. I do not necessarily believe the dream can be realised in its fulness, but I'd like to think it might have inspired you to reach out and embrace your potential to change the lives of the people around you for the better.

Many dream of a life that does not involve work. A life lived at leisure, without worries or responsibilities. My dream is more mundane. Mine is a dream of a working life well lived. They say that, if we are fortunate enough to live until we are 80, we will spend a third of our lives at work. They also say we spend a third of our lives asleep. Which means that half of our waking lives are spent at work. That is a lot of opportunity to live well.

Frankl suggested that a meaningful life is found in taking responsibility to answer life's questions and fulfil life's tasks.[1] He reminds us that everything is transitory and that a life well lived is not lived in past glories or future riches. Meaningfulness is found in simply living day by day, moment by moment. It is in turning up as ourselves with the intent to make a positive difference to those around us.

I dream of workplaces where people feel seen and valued for who they are. Working lives in which together we enter into that profound contract to see and be seen. Where we experience belonging and safety in healthy workplace communities.

I dream of more teams discovering the joy that comes when they truly understand the potential that is unlocked when they turn up for each other. I dream of workplace communities in which people flourish in the knowledge of what they can achieve together and dream of changing the world for the better.

My hope is that, in some small way, this book has shifted your perspective, opened your eyes, or just given a sense of how much we need you to be you. How you are uniquely positioned to make a positive difference to the people around you.

At the heart of the organisation in which you work is a complex human system capable of delivering amazing outcomes, for your clients, for your colleagues and for the community. In turn those human systems we call businesses are just nodes in the unfathomably complex system in which we all live. The complexity may be beyond us, but the implications are simple:

- We need each other.
- Our ability to flourish is intimately connected.
- Everything you are and everything you achieve is thanks to others.
- We need you to turn up having chosen to be the difference that will enable others to flourish.

This is our moment to turn up and be the difference: one moment, one choice, one connection at a time.

Be you and make the difference

Try this thought experiment:

You have just invested a significant amount of time reading this book. Before you move on to the next book in your reading list, take a moment to reflect.

What will you do differently having read this book?

How are you going to turn up for your family, in your workplace community, for wider society?

How will you make sure to take your self to work?

What commitment will you make to your self to make sure you retain the value you've got from this book?

ENDNOTES

1 Viktor E. Frankl, *Man's search for meaning*, 2004, Penguin, p.85

Access your bonus material

Visit www.turning-up.co.uk to access your bonus material.

- Recommended reading that will take you deeper into the topics explored in each chapter.
- Worksheets for various exercises that will enable you to explore what it means for you to take your self to work.

If you are in business leadership, there are also bonus chapters with ideas on how you can create a healthy workplace community.

Use the QR code below to visit turning-up.co.uk and claim your bonus material.

Acknowledgements

This book captures a fifteen-year personal journey of discovery. In January 2023, to encourage myself to put my thoughts on paper I gathered a small group of people who would help me clarify my thinking and give me feedback on my early drafts: Nathan McNamara , Jaccy Datta, Susan Reznik, Ben Calvert-Lyons and Wendy Furness – thank you for your early encouragement and the time you gave me.

I'd also like to thank others who have challenged my thinking and supported me on my personal journey this far. In particular: Simon Hague, Myles Downey, Richard Merrick and Andrew Curwen.

Finally, I'd like to thank my business partner Robert Heed for his belief in me, and the support and encouragement as we have built Growhouse together.

About Ian Harrison

I spend my time partnering with business leaders as they build healthy communities that deliver their business objectives.

Since having made a significant career change in 2010, I've been coaching senior leaders, and developing bespoke learning opportunities designed to enable my clients' businesses to achieve their objectives, whilst creating opportunity for their people to thrive.

In 2023 I partnered with world leading coach, Myles Downey, to write *The Enabling Manager*. That book has opened opportunities to meet amazing leaders, and work with brilliant teams as they develop the communication skills required to enable people to live their best life at work whilst delivering outstanding results for their businesses.

A longstanding client once described my approach as walking with them through the landscape, helping them to unpick their thoughts and opening new doors to other interesting places. I don't see myself as a trainer but as someone who will introduce you to models and ideas that will enrich your thinking and enable you to find your way to the outcomes you want.

I'm a proud Lancastrian who has spent his entire adult life living in and around the West Midlands. Having grown up in Blackburn, I'm a lifelong Blackburn Rovers fan and you'll often find me in the Riverside Stand at Ewood Park in one of my many blue and white shirts. I'm also a proud father and grandfather.

I'd love to connect with you. Use the QR code below to find me on LinkedIn or visit www.Turning-up.co.uk

BV - #0045 - 120126 - C0 - 203/127/12 - PB - 9781908770967 - Matt Lamination